DERBYSHIRE GUIDE

EDITED BY
Robert Innes-Smith

BENE CONSULENDO

CONTENTS

A map of the county and a list of youth hostels and caravan sites will be found on the inside back cover.

D1340883

Opposite: Alport Stone

nt Cover: Millstones on Stanage Edge

Back Cover: Chee Dale

DERBYSHIRE – A WORLD IN ITSELF

Apart from a coastline and natural lakes, Derbyshire is a microcosm of England and you will find in Derbyshire a cross-section of the characteristics of most other English counties – mountains; dales; rivers whose beauty is renowned; some of the most spectacular caverns in Britain; more than its fair share of distinguished and beautiful country houses; historic towns; houses and places associated with famous people; some of the best scenery and walking country in Britain; locations for rock-climbing, pot-holing, gliding, canoeing, yachting and other sports and a rich variety of customs dating from time immemorial.

Derbyshire may not have access to the sea nor to natural lakes but there are several large and beautiful reservoirs in the county – centres of leisure pursuits such as boating, fishing and wind surfing.

The City of Derby is synonymous with household names such as Rolls-Royce and Royal Crown Derby fine porcelain and has been a major railway centre since 1847. It has also given its name to one of the greatest painters of the 18th century – Joseph Wright known as 'Wright of Derby'. The county has associa-tions with famous writers – Izaak Walton, George Eliot, D. H. Lawrence, Dr. Johnson and the Sitwell family.

The Peak National Park is one of Britain's most famous areas of outstanding beauty with public access to large tracts of it.

There are some phenomena unique to Derbyshire – the rare mineral bluejohn, the old and mysterious custom of well-dressing and Mam Tor – 'the shivering mountain'. Where else would you find an American theme park or the sort of experience to be had on the Heights of Abraham, a micrarium or a grotesquely twisted church spire?

Derbyshire was, and to some extent still is, the centre of industrial England. It is also the cradle of the Industrial Revolution and contains many reminders of some of the men who brought it about such as Brindley, Arkwright and Strutt. There are numerous relics of this great industrial past throughout the county from old lead mines to water mills.

Whether you are a walker, climber, pot-holer, antiquarian, historian, sportsman or simply enjoy tootling about sight-seeing, Derbyshire has it all.

Derwent Reservoir. Opposite: entrance to Peak Cavern, Castleton

WHERE TO GO – WHAT TO SEE

Opening times occasionally change so verification of all such information throughout this book is recommended.

ALTON – *Alton Towers*
This famous place is in Staffordshire. Alton Towers has a duel personality. On the one hand it comprises the enormous, mainly ruinous former home of the Earls of Shrewsbury with beautiful rock and rose gardens, tree-lined valley slopes; rhododendron walks; woodland walks; follies; a pagoda and conservatories. On the other hand, out of sight of all this beauty is another world – 'where wonders never cease'. Here is the famous 'Corkscrew' – a terrifying double loop and the even more frightening 'Thunder Looper' which catapults out of its station and reaches 60 m.p.h. in 2.8 seconds. Then there is Cine 2000, a circus on ice, a Grand Canyon rapids ride and a sky ride where you can pass from one aspect of Alton Towers to the other far above for a bird's eye view. There are many other attractions which make this place one of the biggest magnets in the Midlands.

Above: Alton Towers

Left: Old House Museum, Bakewell

BAKEWELL – *Old House Museum*
A 16th century house retaining many original features in spite of having been converted to a row of cottages by Sir R. Arkwright. Now restored and housing Victorian kitchen, 19th century costume display, craftsmen's tools, toys and many other exhibits. Open afternoons 1st April-31st October. (telephone 0629 813647).

BURTON-UPON-TRENT – *Bass Museum*
A museum celebrating one of the great names in brewing, with locomotives, steam engines, historic motor and horse-drawn vehicles and Bass shire horses. There are conference and exhibition facilities and a visitors' centre. (telephone 0283 511000).

BURTON-ON-TRENT – *Heritage Brewery Museum*
Situated in Anglesey Road, Burton, this is a 19th century brewery restored and working. The whole brewery together with its cottages, stabling and waggon sheds form England's first independent working brewery museum. You can see the various stages of the brewing process and a free glass of ale is provided for all adult visitors. (telephone 0283 69226).

BUTTERLEY – *Midland Railway Centre*
This is centred on Butterley Station, demolished after the Beeching closures but now completely rebuilt using the stones from another derelict station. There are 57 acres of museum buildings and exhibits together with a country park.
This is a working railway museum with a line running from Butterley to Ironville, with steam locomotives regularly making the journey and pulling passenger carriages. (telephone 0773 747674).

BUXTON – *Micrarium*, The Crescent, Buxton
The world's first Micrarium. An exhibition of Nature under the microscope. Snowflakes, feathers, flower buds, live pond water specimens, minerals and crystals which can be melted and watched growing again under polarised light forming colourful kaleidoscopic patterns. Open daily from March 23rd-November 10th, 10 a.m.-5 p.m. and some winter week-ends (please telephone for details). (telephone 0298 78662.

BUXTON – *Buxton Museum and Art Gallery*, Terrace Road
This won the 1990 National Heritage Museum of the Year award for the best museum of archaeological or historical interest. The Wonders of the Peak Galleries feature the archaeology, geology and history of the Peak. (telephone 0298 24658).

BUXTON – *Peak Rail Steam Centre*, Midland Station
Open all the year, Monday to Friday 9 a.m.-5 p.m.; Saturdays and Sundays 11 a.m.-5 p.m.. Steam rides available, Easter to October on Sundays and Bank Holidays. (telephone 0298 79898).

CASTLETON – *Blue John Museum*
This museum houses the Ollerenshaw Collection, one of the largest collections of blue john in the world. (telephone 0433 20642).

CASTLETON – *Castleton Village Museum*, Methodist School Hall
A museum of local history and geology with wheelwright and blacksmith workshops and other displays.

CHESTERFIELD – *Queens Park Sports Centre*
A fine Victorian park offering band concerts; boating; bowling; cricket; a miniature railway; children's play

area; tennis courts and a lake. The Sports Centre hosts regional and national sporting events.

CRESWELL – *Creswell Crags*
A limestone gorge once the home of early man. The visitor centre has a shop and audio-visual programme. There is a woodland walk and a lake. Whaley Thorns Heritage Centre – see p. 7. (telephone 0909 720378).

CRICH – *National Tramway Museum*
A working museum of trams at Crich where immaculately restored tramcars from Sheffield, Edinburgh, Blackpool and other places at home and overseas cater for passengers. In all are some 40 vintage horse-drawn, electric and steam trams built between 1873

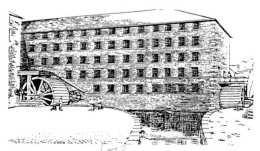

and 1953. Trams run every few minutes for a two-mile scenic round trip. Visitors are advised to check opening times beforehand. Admission charge. Free parking. (telephone 077 385 2565).

CROMFORD – *Arkwright's Cromford Mill*
This important piece of industrial archaeology the world's first successful water powered cotton spinning mill – in effect the first factory – is gradually being reinstated. Guided tours, an audio-visual display and exhibitions about Arkwright and cotton spinning are part of the service here and there are shops and a cafe. The site is open daily. (telephone 0629 824297).

CROMFORD – *Leawood Pumphouse*
A restored beam engine dating from 1849 used to pump water into the Cromford Canal from the River Derwent. For details of opening times please telephone 0629 823204/822831.

CROMFORD – *Cromford Wharf Steam Museum*
A collection of industrial steam engines open by appointment only. (telephone 0629 823727).

CROMFORD – *High Peak Junction Workshops*
Restored workshops of the old Cromford and High Peak Railway with an exhibition, shop and information centre. Picnicking allowed by the canal. (telephone 0629 822831).

DARLEY DALE – *Red House Stables Carriage Museum*, Old Road
A display of horse-drawn carriages and their accoutrements. Many of the exhibits are in regular use and carriages and a four-in-hand coach can be hired. (telephone 0629 733583).

DENBY – *Denby Pottery Visitors' Centre*
Denby Pottery is situated in the village of Denby two miles south of Ripley and 8 miles north of Derby on the B6179.

See the potters in action or visit the museum to see Denby pots new and old. Find a bargain in the Site Shop or just enjoy a light meal in the Potter's Wheel restaurant. Denby Visitors' Centre is open 7 days a week. (telephone 0773 743641).

DERBY – *Pickford's House, 41 Friar Gate*
This was built by the architect Joseph Pickford for himself as a family home in 1770. It is now part of Derby Museum and is open to the public. The rooms have been furnished in the manner appropriate to a Georgian professional man with figures in costume of the time. (telephone Derby 255363).

Opening Hours: Monday 11.00 a.m.-5.00 p.m. Tuesday-Saturday 10.00 a.m.-5.00 p.m. Sunday & Bank Holidays 2.00 p.m.-5.00 p.m. Admission: Small charge. Sundays free.

Above left: Crich Tramway Museum showing the re-sited facade of the old Derby Assembly Rooms and Crich Stand in the distance

Right: the classical front door of Pickford's House, Friargate

Left: Arkwright's Mill

DERBY – *Museums and Art Gallery, Wardwick*
Museum: antiques, bygones, coins and medals, zoology, geology, Bonnie Prince Charlie Room. Art Gallery: paintings by Joseph Wright of Derby, Derby porcelain, and frequent temporary exhibitions. School service and holiday activities for children. Admission free. (telephone Derby 293111).

DERBY – *Museum of Industry and Technology*
Silk Mill, Full Street, Derby
Rolls-Royce aero engine collection, a Power for Industry display and a Railway Gallery with scale model of Midland Railway layout, and other displays relating to the principal industries of Derby and Derbyshire. Admission free. (telephone Derby 293111).

DERBY – *Royal Crown Derby Museum,*
Osmaston Road
A display of this famous porcelain from 1752 onwards. There are two factory tours a day beginning at 10.30 a.m. and 1.45 p.m. each lasting about 1½ hours. (telephone 0332 47051)

ELVASTON – *The Working Estate,* Elvaston Castle. See page 13.

ILKESTON – *The American Adventure*
Situated in Shipley Park (eight clearly signposted miles for Junction 26 of the M1), you can lose yourself in the Wild West with gun fights, a train, shooting the rapids, jazz bands, in all over 100 rides, attractions and live-action events including big dipper rides and boat trips on the lake. (telephone 0773 531521).

ILKESTON – *Erewash Museum,* High Street
An 18th century and mid-Victorian town house displaying local items of social, industrial and domestic interest. (telephone 0602 440440 ext. 331).

MATLOCK BATH – *Gulliver's Kingdom*
This is one of Matlock Bath's many attractions set in the hillside. It contains a wide range of activities for families – a Wild West experience, a Dinosaur Walk, little Switzerland, with shops, restaurants and an hotel. Other attractions include a guest house; a Log Flume; puppet shows; a water garden; a log roller coaster; veteran cars and many more. (telephone 0629 580540).

Cable cars at the Heights of Abraham, Matlock Bath

MATLOCK BATH – *The Heights of Abraham*
The cable cars high above the A6 will take you from the River Derwent to the country park at the summit of the Heights of Abraham, where visitors can enter two of Derbyshire's great caverns, call at the Visitor Centre and enjoy some of the best panoramic views in the Midlands. There is a licensed restaurant and bar, a coffee shop and a gift shop, and woodland walks lead to picnic areas and the Prospect Tower. There is also a gift shop set amongst the streams, waterfalls and pools. (telephone 0629 582365).

MATLOCK BATH – *Aquarium,* North Parade
On site of orginal thermal pool. Collection of cold water, tropical and marine fish. Open April-October daily 10 a.m.-6 p.m. Winter weekends 11 a.m.-5.30 p.m. (telephone 0629 583624).

MATLOCK BATH – *Temple Mine.*
A reconstructed working lead and fluorite mine typifying a mine of the 1900s. (telephone 0629 583834).

PINXTON – *John King's Workshop Museum,* Victoria Road
This features John King's invention for mine cages plus old mining equipment, obsolete household utensils and a display of historic industrial photographs. (telephone 0773 810238/860137/860179.

RIBER – *Riber Castle Wildlife Park*
The home of rare and endangered species of animals and birds in the grounds of the dramatic ruins of Riber Castle near Matlock Bath. Open all the year. (telephone 0629 2073). N.B. Check before visiting.

RIPLEY – *Midland Railway Centre* – see Butterley

ROWSLEY – *Caudwell's Mill Craft Centre*
The largest craft shop in the county. Five craft workshops and glass-blowing studio. Gallery of distinctive work. Working, water-powered flour mill. Country parlour, wholefood home-baking and beautiful views. (telephone 0629 733185).

SHARDLOW – *Hoskin's Wharf*
This building, over 200 years old, was formerly the Clock Warehouse housing a canal museum. It is now a 90-seater restaurant with two bars open 7 days a week throughout the year for lunches and dinners. (telephone Derby 792844).

SUDBURY – *Museum of Childhood*
This museum is at the time of writing housed in Sudbury Hall but please see page 22.

VIA GELLIA – *Good Luck Mine*
A working lead mine of the mid 19th century with an underground lead-mining museum. (telephone 0246 72375).

WEST HALLAM – *The Bottle Kiln,* High Lane West (A609)
A unique historic bottle-necked kiln is here the centrepoint for a fine art gallery, craft shop and buttery café. Open Tuesday to Sunday 10 a.m. to 5 p.m. (telephone 0602 392442).

WHITTINGTON – *Revolution House*
This is three miles north of Chesterfield at Old Whittington. Formerly the Cock and Pynot Inn, this 17th century cottage was the place where the Earls of Devonshire and Danby and John D'Arcy planned their part in the Bloodless Revolution of 1688 to ensure the Protestant Succession by calling over William of Orange to be King in place of James II.

Display and video. Open Saturdays and Sundays all the year round, daily Easter to October.

WIRKSWORTH – *National Stone Centre*
This is an exhibition telling the story of stone from pre-historic tool-making to modern techniques. Outside can be seen 300 million-year-old fossil reefs, mines and quarries. (telephone 0629 824833).

HERITAGE CENTRES

GLOSSOP HERITAGE CENTRE –
Norfolk Square, Glossop
Illustrates many aspects of the town from Roman to Victorian times. Contains an Art Gallery and Victorian Kitchen. (telephone 0457 869176).

NEW MILLS HERITAGE CENTRE –
New Mills
This is at the confluence of the Rivers Sett and Goyt and contains displays illustrating the history and evolution of New Mills. Regular exhibitions are put on and there is a model of a mine for children to explore. Refreshments available. Open every day except Monday. (telephone 0663 746904).

PEACOCK HERITAGE CENTRE –
Low Pavement, Chesterfield
Housed in a fine medieval half-timbered house with changing exhibitions of regional interest. The Centre

is also a tourist information office and shop. (telephone 0246 207777).

WHALEY THORNS HERITAGE CENTRE – Langwith
Geological displays including minerals and gemstones together with international handicrafts. Headquarters of the Cresswell Heritage Trust (see page 5). (telephone 0623 742525).

WIRKSWORTH HERITAGE CENTRE –
off the Market Place
This splendid panorama of Wirksworth's long history is housed in what was once a derelict silk mill. H.R.H. the Princess Margaret visited in June 1984 as the builders were starting and it opened on 17th May 1986. It has a very good restaurant and there is a sales point. (telephone 0629 825225).

THEATRES

Those who live in Derbyshire are well served for theatres as however far from Derby they might live, there are theatres in neighbouring counties within reach.

DERBY. *The Derby Playhouse* (telephone 363275) is in the Eagle Centre and is a very popular place with plenty of every kind of drama.

BUXTON. The magnificently restored *Opera House* (telephone 0298 72190) puts on ballet, opera, orchestral concerts and plays.

CHESTERFIELD. The *Pomegranate Theatre* (telephone 0246 232901) is in Corporation Street.

LEICESTER. Leicester's *Haymarket Theatre* (telephone 0533 539797) is in Belgrave Gate.

MANCHESTER. This city has: the *Royal Exchange Theatre* (telephone 061 833 9833) in St. Ann's Square; the *Library Theatre* (telephone 061 236 7110) in St. Peter's Square; the *Palace Theatre* (telephone 061 236 9922) in Oxford Road; the *Opera House* (telephone 061 831 7766) in Quay Street, and the *Contact Theatre* (telephone 061 274 4400).

NEWCASTLE-UNDER-LYME. The *New Victoria Theatre* (telephone 0782 717962) is in Etruria Road.

NOTTINGHAM. The *Theatre Royal* (telephone 97 482626) in Theatre Square is Nottingham's traditional surviving Victorian theatre. The *Nottingham Playhouse* (telephone 97 419419) in Wellington Circus is, in contrast, very modern while the *Lacemarket Theatre* (telephone 97 507201) is a centre for amateur dramatics.

SHEFFIELD. The *Lyceum* (telephone 0742 769922) in Norfolk Street is Sheffield's newly restored Victorian theatre and the *Crucible Theatre* (telephone 0742 769922) has a wide reputation.

Calke Abbey

CALKE ABBEY *Map N.7*

BUILT IN 1703 for Sir John Harpur to replace his old seat at Swarkestone, Calke is the second largest house in Derbyshire with, among others, architects Gibbs, Smith of Warwick and Wilkins associated with it.

Here, until the 1980s, when the house was acquired by the National Trust, lingered the last echoes of the 19th century, not in any contrived museum reconstruction but simply because the family had never allowed the 20th century into the domains. And who could blame them? Sir Vauncey Harpur-Crewe (1846-1924) would not even allow horseless carriages into the park. Motor cars had to be left at the park gates and a horse-drawn vehicle from the stables would be sent to collect the visitor. His distrust of the internal combustion engine showed what a sensible and far-sighted man he was!

Not only was the 20th century kept at bay but the relics of previous centuries were never banished. Although, inevitably, motor cars were eventually allowed in, more leisurely forms of transport were never discarded. Thus to this day barouches and landaus are still in the stables, together with ancient bicycles and even a wheeled bier for transporting dead squires to the churchyard.

It is still the case that when you enter the park through the somewhat unprepossessing gates in Ticknall, the centuries roll away and you are back in the age of Stubbs and Ferneley. Regency England stretches before you as far as the eye can see. The drive is nearly two miles long and glimpses can be

The Saloon

The Gold Drawing Room survives with all its Victorian hugger mugger

had not only of deer and game but also of fragments of woodland as old as Sherwood Forest where age has sculpted the oaks into fantastic shapes. As you approach the huge classical house and its stables you half expect to see the scurry of ostlers and grooms to meet you and release your horses from their traces, or spy the estate carpenter or the blacksmith, aproned and smutty in the stable yard. For although no-one appears, all the tools are there – the forge, the joiner's shop, the tack room and the carriages.

Calke is a colossal house and one thing the family was not short of was room. If a change of scene was required, rooms would be shut up and others occupied. Some closed rooms never seemed to have been opened again until recently. When Sir Vauncey brought a bride to Calke in 1876 (he was the last squire to do so) he shut up his own bachelor bedroom containing the stuffed heads of deer he shot as a boy together with his collection of butterflies and moved to a more suitable chamber. His old room remained dust-laden and neglected, the clutter of a Victorian boyhood strewn upon floor and bed.

Inside, the rooms have been carefully restored, leaving them, visually, as close to what they were when the Trust took over. The Victorian clutter remains and the Drawing Room, the great Saloon (Calke's most impressive room), and other rooms are as they were when Calke and other great country houses were in their heyday. The 'new' four-poster bed, not long out of its 18th century packing case, is a wondrous survival.

Strange quirks of inheritance had much to do with the fate of the house and estate. Sir Vauncey's only son and heir pre-deceased him and at his own death one of his daughters, Mrs. Mosley, inherited the estate.

In the fullness of time, Sir Vauncey's younger daughter's son, Mr. Charles Jenney, inherited Calke and assumed the name and arms of Harpur-Crewe. He was a bachelor and was succeeded by his bachelor brother, Mr. Henry Harpur-Crewe whose tremendous efforts resulted in the transfer of ownership of the house and surroundings to the National Trust, which now administers it. Mr. Harpur-Crewe still lives in the house which is open from the end of March to the end of October, Saturdays to Wednesdays and Bank Holidays.

Chatsworth, the West Front. Opposite: the Library

CHATSWORTH *Map F.5*

EVEN AS long ago as the days of Thomas Hobbes, Chatsworth has been accounted one of the Wonders of the Peak. In Hobbes's day the building was Elizabethan, built by the 1st Earl of Devonshire's mother, Bess of Hardwick. This huge pile was replaced by the 4th Earl after he had been elevated to become 1st Duke of Devonshire for his part in the 'Bloodless Revolution' of 1688. The designs for the new house may well have been drawn up by the Duke himself (he was a man of taste and education) though both Thomas Archer and Talman were involved. As the latter architect was sacked in 1696, it looks as if the Duke may well have designed the West Front which is by far the best elevation. The Duke also employed some very talented craftsmen to embellish his palace – painters Sir James Thornhill, Louis Laguerre and Antonio Verrio, Caius Gabriel Cibber, the sculptor, and the celebrated French ironsmith André Tijou.

The carving in the State Rooms is famous and was carried out not by Grinling Gibbons as old guides to the house used to say, but by London carvers Young, Lobb and Davis, though the principal carver was a local man, Samuel Watson, who joined the London trio in 1689 and eventually surpassed them as a master craftsman in both wood and stone.

In Bess of Hardwick's day the principal front had been the East, but the 1st Duke re-orientated the house so that the West Front was paramount. The 4th Duke and his architect James Paine, probably under the influence of the Duke's father-in-law, that 18th century Maecenas, Lord Burlington, built the bridge over the Derwent and the gargantuan stables (his arms and those of his Burlington heiress wife can be seen carved over the entrance) and landscaped the surrounding park with the aid of the ubiquitous Lancelot 'Capability' Brown.

The 6th Duke devoted most of his life to improving Chatsworth. His head gardener, Joseph Paxton (later to achieve international fame for his designs for the Great Exhibition of 1851 and a knighthood), was responsible for the present appearance of the garden. The Duke employed Sir Jeffry Wyatville (George IV's architect at Windsor Castle) to build the long north wing terminating in the Theatre Tower and to carry out many improvements to the main block.

In this century, the 9th Duke and his architect W. H. Romaine-Walker, greatly improved the Painted Hall.

There is nothing new in the public being allowed over Chatsworth – visitors have enjoyed its bucolic pleasures without and the intellectual feasts within for generations, none more so than in the last decades of the twentieth century.

The 6th Duke of Devonshire

The Cascade House

The Library contains one of the greatest private collections of books, prints and Old Master drawings in the world. The Sculpture Gallery contains magnificent specimens from classical times to the present and throughout the incomparable · rooms are paintings, tapestries and fine pieces of furniture second to none. What is of special satisfaction is that the Duke of Devonshire, whose forbears built the house and collected the contents over four centuries,

lives in the house with the Duchess (née Mitford), and, like their predecessors, members of the family play an important role in county affairs. The Duke, a man well-known in the racing world, has used his winnings to add to Chatsworth's treasures with examples of both ancient and modern art.

In 1973 the Farmyard was opened to give visitors an insight into how the farms and woodlands on the estate are run and there is a farm shop at near-by Pilsley. The public is also allowed access to certain parts of the park including the Stand Wood Walks in the vicinity of the Hunting Tower.

From time to time events take place in the house and park, and there is a children's adventure playground.

Chatsworth is open approximately from April to October with its garden and farm. The garden and shop also open on Sundays during part of the winter. For information apply to: The Comptroller, Chatsworth House, Bakewell. (telephone 0246 582204).

Sir Joseph Paxton

Down on the farm – at Chatsworth Farmyard

ELVASTON CASTLE *Map M.8*

THE HUGE park and its castle was the seat of a junior branch of the Stanhope family, the Earls of Harrington, from the 16th century to the 1930s when Lord Harrington left Derbyshire to live in Ireland. He sold the estate and in 1969 it eventually came into the joint ownership of Derbyshire County Council and Derby Borough Council. It is now a country park and, with the gardens and part of the house, is open all the year round to the public.

The Harrington Stanhopes were a branch of the Earls of Chesterfield who lived at Bretby.

The south front of Elvaston shows part of the old house built of brick and dating from 1633. In 1817 it was remodelled in the Gothick style to designs by James Wyatt. The old house was clad in ashlar and castellated to make it into a 'castle'. Some of the interiors are extravagantly Gothick with fan-vaulting and heraldry.

The park has long vistas and rides, one culminating in the famous Golden Gates, removed by Napoleon from a royal palace in Madrid and taken to France. The gates were eventually acquired by the Stanhopes and re-erected here suitably embellished with the coronet of an English earl and the Stanhope arms.

The most remarkable thing about Elvaston is the garden which was designed by William Barron who was commissioned by the 4th Earl in 1830 to lay out the grounds. Barron was associated with the project for some twenty years. There is much topiary and also *rocaille* – the artifical rock formations made from volcanic tufa rock which so impressed the Duke of Wellington. There is also a riding school in the stables and a lake inhabited by many waterfowl.

Since the late 1960s the County Council has been working on a complete restoration of the gardens which had suffered neglect when the Stanhopes left.

Also in the grounds is the Working Estate Museum of country life with craftsmen and estate workshops reconstructing domestic scenes of Edwardian England and a collection of farm vehicles.

For further information telephone Derby 571342.

Haddon Hall, the garden front

HADDON HALL *Map F.5*

HADDON HALL is everyone's idea of an old English country house. Much of it dates from the fourteenth and fifteenth centuries and is thus a relic of the Age of Chivalry. It owes its extraordinary state of preservation, ironically, to neglect. For generations it remained empty, though not quite a ruin. Its 'Gothick' appearance attracted artists and poets and even an opera was written around it by Sir Arthur Sullivan. Haddon thus survived the modish architectural foibles of succeeding ages until, like some sleeping beauty, it was given the kiss of life by the 9th Duke of Rutland during the 1920s.

The Manners family inherited Haddon after John Manners, brother of the 2nd Earl of Rutland, married Dorothy one of the co-heiresses of Sir George Vernon 'King of the Peak', the last Vernon of Haddon Hall. Legend has it that Manners eloped with Dorothy Vernon, but there would seem to be no reason why this should be and it has never been proved. The Vernons had lived at Haddon for four centuries inheriting it from the Avenels who came there in 1153. Thus the present Duke of Rutland holds the property in direct descent from that date.

The magnificent Banqueting Hall is 14th century and the Long Gallery with its Renaissance panelling and diamond-pane windows, contains a large

Below left: the approach to Haddon Hall

Below: Haddon's Great Chamber

Haddon's medieval Banqueting Hall

painting by Rex Whistler of the 9th Duke and his son, the 10th Duke.

The Chapel has medieval wall paintings and a fine marble monument to a young boy – Lord Haddon, the son of Violet Duchess of Rutland (he was the older brother of the 9th Duke). The Duchess herself designed the monument which has roundel portraits of other members of the family, including Lady Diana Manners, better known as Lady Diana Cooper.

The story of Haddon and its architecture is too long to embark on here, but it is all well set out in the guide book.

The house is open to the public at regular times during the summer months. For details apply to: The Curator, Estate Office, Haddon Hall, Bakewell (telephone 0629 812855).

HARDWICK HALL *Map G.9*

LIKE BOLSOVER, Hardwick Hall is unique of its kind. Its gleaming towers now look as new as the day they were built, thanks to the National Trust (which now owns the house) having cleaned the stonework. In the process much of the mystery endowed by the grimy patina of age has vanished with the dirt.

Although Elizabethan, Hardwick is curiously modern in aspect particularly in relationship to the proportion of window to wall. The famous 'more glass than wall' tag is true, which is why the great rooms within are so light and airy.

The stone initials ES and the coronet proclaim the builder – Bess of Hardwick, matriarch of the Derbyshire gentry. Elizabeth Hardwick had four husbands, the last being the 6th Earl of Shrewsbury (hence the initials). Her second husband was Sir William Cavendish, the only one by whom she had children. By dint of her genetic 'engineering' many noble and gentle families descend from her. Not only did Bess build families, she is also known for building houses. She built the first Chatsworth House, then rebuilt her old modest ancestral home Hardwick Hall. The ruins of this house still stand close to the present, even grander, replacement which she completed towards the end of her life. There were others, too, but none remains in its original form except Hardwick.

Along with Chatsworth, Hardwick passed to her second son, William Cavendish afterwards 1st Earl of Devonshire. It remained a dower house of the Devonshire family until recently and thus escaped architectural changes. The last member of the family to live there was Evelyn Duchess of Devonshire, grandmother of the present Duke. She did much to gather together from other of the family houses objects which properly belonged to Hardwick and to remove other items which did not.

Bess of Hardwick's armorial chimneypiece at Hardwick

The ruins of Hardwick Old Hall

The interiors are amongst the most exciting in England, particularly the High Great Chamber and the Long Gallery. The collection of tapestry and needlework of the period is second to none. Hardwick Hall is open to the public at regular times during the summer months. For details apply to: The Administrator, Hardwick Hall, nr. Chesterfield (telephone Chesterfield 850430).

Hardwick's famous High Great Chamber

Robert Adam's South Front of Kedleston Hall. Opposite: the Marble Hall

KEDLESTON HALL *Map L.6*

KEDLESTON HALL was the last-built of the great houses of Derbyshire. The successor of at least two other large buildings on the same site occupied by members of the Curzon family since Henry I's reign about 850 years ago, it was erected in the 1760s by Sir Nathaniel Curzon, the first Baron Scarsdale, whose descendant, Viscount Scarsdale, is the present occupant. The first mention of the church is in the first of the ancient Curzon deeds dated 10 Richard I, i.e. about 6 July, 1198, when Richard de Curzon granted the Village and Manor of Kedleston, or Ketelstune as it was then spelt, with the advowson of the Church, to Thomas, son of Thomas de Curzun, his grandson. The Hall is a noble example of the work – both exterior and interior – of Robert Adam, though not all the credit for its design can be given to him. Two other architects, Matthew Brettingham and James Paine, were employed on the work before he was called in. The north front is by Paine; the south by Adam.

Within, the most splendid room is the Marble Hall, which must rank only after the High Great Chamber at Hardwick among the most magnificent apartments in the county. Rows of 25 ft high pink alabaster columns surround the room. They are of stone from quarries at Red Hill, in Nottinghamshire. The floor is of Italian marble and Derbyshire Hopton Wood stone.

The state rooms are of great magnificence and filled with important paintings and furniture, much of the latter designed for the house. The Scarsdale family live in the east pavilion.

Until the middle of the eighteenth century, the village of Kedleston was clustered around the Hall, but Sir Nathaniel Curzon had it removed to its present site some distance away. He also had the main road diverted, so that it should not pass too near to the new house. The church, however, remained and it is well worth a visit. It dates in large part from the late thirteenth century or early fourteenth century, although there is much later work, as well as one feature – the Norman south doorway – which is earlier. Of great interest to most visitors is the Curzon Chapel and the monument to Marquess Curzon of Kedleston (1859-1925) a former Viceroy of India, and his first wife.

The house and grounds which now belong to the National Trust, are open to the public at certain times during the summer months. For details apply to: The Curator, Kedleston Hall, Derby. (telephone Derby 842191).

Melbourne Hall and its formal garden. Opposite: Robert Bakewell's famous 'Birdcage'

MELBOURNE HALL *Map N.7*

MELBOURNE HALL, formerly a seat of the Marquis of Lothian, Chief of Clan Kerr, and now the home of his younger son and daughter-in-law Lord and Lady Ralph Kerr, is the most homely of the great houses of Derbyshire. It is full of fine furniture and paintings, and rich in historical associations. The gardens are among the most notable in the country.

The Hall, originally the old rectory occupied by the Bishops of Carlisle, was in 1628 leased by Sir John Coke, a Secretary of State to Charles I, who converted it for use as his own home, using in the process stones from the old Castle of Melbourne, then in a ruinous state. Sir John's great-grandson, Sir Thomas Coke, who came to live at the Hall in 1696, rebuilt part of the house, giving it its main façade on the east front: this is obviously of later date than the rest of the building. Sir Thomas also replanned and enlarged the gardens taking for the purpose the advice of George London and Henry Wise, the two foremost gardeners of the time.

A most interesting feature of the gardens is the wrought-iron arbour made about 1710 by Robert Bakewell, the famous Derby ironsmith, and recently restored. A great domed cage (known locally as 'The Birdcage') is one of the supreme examples of the blacksmith's craft and is unique.

All phases of Melbourne Hall's history are represented in the collection of family portraits and relics which it contains. Sir John Coke, elderly, bearded, beruffed, is here in a portrait by Cornelius Janssens, and Sir Thomas Coke, too, an elegant eighteenth century dandy (by Michael Dahl). For a time in the nineteenth century the house belonged to Lord Melbourne, Queen Victoria's first Prime Minister: his portrait is to be seen above his own writing table. The house also had connexions with Lord Palmerston and later passed into the Kerr family, on the marriage of Lady Amabel Cowper and Admiral of the Fleet Lord Walter Kerr, who came to live here in 1906. The estate has passed to Lord Lothian by direct descent from Sir John Coke.

Melbourne Hall is open during August for pre-booked parties and its famous gardens are open from April to September at certain times. For details apply to: The Curator, Melbourne Hall, Derbyshire (telephone 0332 862502).

Entrance to Sudbury Hall. Opposite: the Long Gallery

SUDBURY HALL *Map M.4*

UNTIL RECENT years Sudbury Hall has been less well-known than its more celebrated neighbours in a county rich in great houses mainly because it had never been opened to the public. Yet this mansion is among the most interesting in the Midlands both architecturally and in the richness of its interiors. The house belonged to the Vernon family from 1513 until 1967 when it was accepted by the Treasury in part payment of death duties and transferred to the National Trust, and is now regularly open to the public. (For further information tel. Sudbury 305).

Sudbury Hall was built in two stages during the seventeenth century and was begun by Mary Vernon in 1613 exactly a century after the estate had come into the possession of her family. Building was started from scratch as there was no existing house on the site. The house was enlarged by Mary Vernon's grandson, George Vernon, in 1665 and it is to this man that we owe the upper storey and most of the elaborate interiors which are today the glory of Sudbury.

If Sudbury Hall is a plain house to look at from the outside, its interiors are rich and elaborate. Two London plasterers, Bradbury and Pettifer, did some of their finest work here, Laguerre, the painter, who also worked at Chatsworth, co-operated with these plasterers in the decoration of the ceilings. Two other craftsmen employed during the alterations and additions which took place in the 1660s were Edward Pierce, a highly skilled wood carver and Grinling Gibbons himself. Pierce and Gibbons did most of the woodwork decoration at Sudbury between them. In a house of many fine rooms, perhaps the most important are the long gallery and the main hall with its wonderful staircase. In the park is what looks like a crenellated folly but is, in fact, a decorative deercote.

Queen Adelaide, the widow of William IV, spent some time here after her husband's death and there are mementoes in the house to remind us of this royal connexion.

At the time of writing the fate of the Museum of Childhood in the Victorian wing, one of the best of its kind in the country, is uncertain. Enquiries should be made to Sudbury 305.

There is a reconstructed Victorian schoolroom and a nursery and old toys and games and much else besides.

Lord Vernon's family now lives in a smaller house on the estate.

CAVERNS

BRADWELL

BAGSHAWE CAVERN situated some two miles from Hope. This contains some very beautiful crystalizations and stalactites. Open by appointment. (telephone 0433 21298).

BUXTON

POOLE'S CAVERN, Buxton (in the grounds of Buxton Country Park) – Open most days from Spring to Autumn (check Wednesdays). Special reduced rates for parties booked in advance. Children 4-16 half price. Enquiries to The Warden, Poole's Cavern, Green Lane, Buxton. (telephone 0298 26978).

CASTLETON

BLUE JOHN CAVERNS, at the summit of Treak Cliff, are where the Blue John Spar has been mined for hundreds of years, and the caverns show a remarkable likeness to Gothic architecture. The vast caverns are reached easily on foot and display many beautiful examples of natural rock formation, sparkling crystal, a cascade of stalagmites, dazzling pendant stalactites, the magnificent coloured dome and rich, variegated rock colouring in spacious chambers. There are said to be at least two miles of passages and caves which are not usually accessible to the ordinary visitor. So involved are the passages and openings of the Blue John that there must be many places, once known and then forgotten with the passage of time, still awaiting rediscovery. Open most days throughout the year, check times in winter. (telephone 0433 20638).

PEAK CAVERN, quite close to the village and under the ruins of Peveril Castle, extends some 2,000 feet underground. Approached through a gorge, it has a path running beside the River Styx and leading through the Five Arches to the Great Chamber, Roger Rain's House and other underground scenes. In the entrance is a remarkable rope-walk, first established in the fifteenth century. Open Easter to end of October daily 10 a.m to 5 p.m. Closed Mondays in low season. Party bookings can be made by schools and youth clubs at reduced rates. (telephone 0433 20285).

TREAK CLIFF CAVERN. Visitors are conducted by guides through two distinct series of caverns. The old series, discovered in 1750 by lead-miners, was found to have the richest deposits of Blue John, England's rarest and most beautiful stone, many veins of which are preserved for visitors to see. Mining operations for Blue John in 1926 resulted in the discovery of a

Stalactites and stalagmites in Treak Cavern

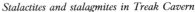

The Blue John Cavern

further series of caves containing what has been described as 'The North of England's finest stalactite caves'. Opened to the public in 1935, the caverns are of very easy access; visitors are shown many chambers, the most outstanding of which are: the Fossil Cave, with its remains from the 330 million year old Carboniferous Period, rich deposits of Blue John in the Witch's Cave, including the Pillar, the largest known piece, weighing over fifteen tons, the multicoloured drapery of stalactites and stalagmites in Aladdin's Cave, the Fairyland Grotto with hundreds of delicate stalactites, and England's finest stalactite chamber, the Dream Cave. Open March–31st October daily 9.30 a.m.-6 p.m. 1st November–28th February daily 9.30 a.m.-4 p.m. (telephone 0433 20571).

SPEEDWELL CAVERN lies under the Winnats and is reached via an old mining tunnel, now partially filled with water. Visitors are taken by boats, along the subterranean canal to the 'Bottomless Pit', where there is said to be an unceasing downpour of water. Open daily all year from 9.30 a.m.-5.30 p.m.

(including Sundays). Free parking. (telephone 0433 20512).

MATLOCK

GREAT MASSON CAVERN, Matlock Bath (in the grounds of the Heights of Abraham) – Open Sundays and Bank Holidays, from Easter to early October, and daily during August from 11 a.m. to 6 p.m., and later in high season.

GREAT RUTLAND CAVERN, Matlock Bath (in the grounds of the Heights of Abraham) – Open daily including Sundays, from Easter to early October, from 10 a.m. to 6 p.m., and later in high season, or at other times by special request.

HIGH TOR GROUNDS, Matlock – Open daily all year 10 a.m. to dusk. Licensed bar, café, children's playground, Roman caves, views of surrounding countryside from the 400 ft. High Tor summit. Picnic areas, woodland walks. Pedestrian access from Matlock Bath, Dale Road, Matlock and Starkholmes. Parties catered for. (telephone 0629 3289).

DERBYSHIRE CUSTOMS

WELL-DRESSING

When Horace, most appealing of all the Roman poets, wrote his famous ode *O fons Bandusiae,* addressing the little spring near his Sabine farm, he may have left us a clue to the antiquity of one of Derbyshire's oldest and most mysterious customs, that of well-dressing. Horace describes the 'chattering waters' as brighter than crystal and says that the well or spring was worthy of gifts of sweet wine *and flowers.* The Romans made regular sacrificial offerings to wells and springs, tinging their cool waters red with blood of goats or bulls but they also made floral tributes. This custom may have been brought to Britain by the Romans and survived mainly in

Coffin Well, Tissington

Derbyshire. Of course a variety of people of antiquity made sacrifices or thank-offerings to their water gods including the ancient Britons and though it is said that nowhere else is well-dressing performed in this way, it has been reported that similar customs still persist in remote parts of Italy. It may suggest that this refinement could indeed have been Roman improvement on more primitive practices in Britain.

After prolonged soaking, wooden frames are filled with damp clay and during the day and night before the tableaux are erected, helpers press in natural colourings (flower petals, leaves, grass, corn, etc.) to fill in pre-determined designs etched onto the smooth, damp clay in the frames. These designs depict biblical scenes, a local church or sometimes

heraldic designs and the results are usually startlingly brilliant. They stand for about a week before being taken down and the frames stored away until the next year.

Wells are dressed at the following places: Ashford-in-the-Water; Ault Hucknall (and Glapwell); Bakewell; Barlborough; Barlow; Baslow; Bonsall; Brackenfield; Bradwell; Buxton; Cutthorpe; Derby (Chester Green); Dore; Elmton; Etwall; Eyam; Hartington; Heath; Holmsfield; Hope; Litton; Monyash; Pilsley (Bakewell); Rowsley; Stoney Middleton; Tideswell; Tissington; Wessington; West Hallam; Whitwell; Wirksworth; Wormhill; Youlgrave.

A list of exact times is published during the appropriate months in *Derbyshire Life and Countryside* and a fully illustrated booklet is available called *Well-Dressing in Derbyshire* by Roy Christian.

GARLAND DAY AT CASTLETON

There is no knowing how long this ceremony has taken place. It may have been as a primitive fertility rite but as in the case of many pre-Christian customs was later adopted to commemorate other things. In this case the *raison d'être* of the ceremony, which takes place on May 29th, is to commemorate the Restoration of Charles II. In living memory 'Oak Apple Day' was once kept by small boys wearing sprigs of oak on their persons. Failure to do so incurred

Parading the garland

punishment by being stung by nettles wielded by more 'loyal' boys, though they probably had no idea why they were doing it.

Garland Day in Castleton is a time of considerable pageantry with people dressing in Stuart fashions and choosing a 'king' and a 'queen' for the day. Processions through the town with a band and morris dancing accompany the ceremony which consists of hoisting a three-foot high garland of flowers to the top of the church tower where it remains for a week.

WINSTER GALLOPS

Although the custom of morris dancing regularly in June in this very attractive village of Winster has lapsed in recent years, another in the form of pancake races on Shrove Tuesday was started after the last war. It can scarcely be numbered among the ancient customs of the county, though it is to be hoped that one day it will be so regarded.

PLAGUE SUNDAY IN EYAM

Everyone knows the tragic story of the Great Plague which ravaged Eyam in 1665, carrying off 259 men, women and children. You cannot visit this lovely village without being reminded of it as one sees pathetic plaques on cottages, or in visiting the churchyard, or in looking at 'Plague Cottage' where it all started. But it is on the last Sunday of every August that the gallant villagers and their two spiritual leaders are remembered in a big ceremony. The villagers were gallant because none left the village in case the pestilence spread but few more so than the Rector, the Rev. William Mompesson and the dissenter he replaced, the Rev. Thomas Stanley, who

Remembrance Service at Cucklet Dell

were the real heroes. They worked tirelessly to relieve suffering and bring comfort to the dying and bereaved. In order to avoid close contact, Mompesson made his parishioners spread out on a grassy dell called Cucklet Dell, now known as 'Cucklet Church' where he would take services. In this same place the remembrance service is held, as it has been on each year since 1905 and in tribute to Stanley, a non-conformist usually reads the lesson, and the choir consists of all denominations. Well-dressing takes place during these proceedings.

WIRKSWORTH CLYPPING AND BARMOTE COURT

Two customs take place in this very ancient town apart from its well-dressing.

The first is the annual 'clypping' of the church which takes place on the nearest Sunday to September 8th. After lapsing for, perhaps, a century, it was revived in 1921. The church was founded in AD 653 and probably stands on a pagan site. Church-goers, after a service in the church, file out of the building and join hands to surround the outside of the building singing 'We love thy place, O Lord, in which Thine honour dwells'. Then there is sometimes a procession through the town joined by

the Bishop or other church dignitaries.

The custom is thought to be a symbolic embracing of the church to show the parishioners' love for the place. A similar custom takes place on the last Sunday in July at Burbage parish church near Buxton.

Another old Wirksworth custom, which takes place twice a year, is the Barmote Court sessions. These relate to disputes over mining rights based upon the ancient custom whereby anyone may mine for minerals in 'The King's Field' – an area covering 115 square miles of Derbyshire irrespective of ownership of the land. This could be done according to set rules and further customs and these are the concern of the Court.

The Great Barmote Court meets in the Moot Hall, a charming 18th century building in the town. Beer, bread and cheese and long-stemmed clay pipes are provided for members of the Court. Jurymen are sworn in and serve for six months. They sit before a famous brass measuring dish dated 1509 and their business is transacted after which they join up for a meal and further smoking.

Lead was one of the main minerals in Derbyshire and particularly in the Wirksworth area and on the wall of the Moot Hall are carved symbols of the lead-mining industry including scales, measuring dish, pickaxe and the 'fasces' a bundle of rods and an axe which were carried before the highest magistrates in ancient Rome and thus in this context the fasces are symbolic of a legal assembly and, perhaps, an allusion to the Romans who mined lead here some sixteen centuries ago.

MAIDENS' GARLANDS

In the days of the old Assize Courts, a visiting judge was sometimes handed a pair of white gloves as a symbol that no crimes had been committed in that area since his last visit. The white glove has often been a symbol of purity and one of Derbyshire's old customs was to hang white paper gloves and 'crantses' or garlands in a church if a virgin of marriageable age died. A girl of similar age and build would precede the coffin carrying the garland which would afterwards hang in the church. Very few of these paper ephemera survive, but they can still be seen in churches at Matlock, Ashford-in-the-Water and Trusley. The garlands or 'crantses' are also made of paper in the form of rosettes draped around young

Maiden's garland at Ashford-in-the-Water

green wooden laths. The word is derived from the German *kranz* meaning a wreath.

ROYAL SHROVETIDE FOOTBALL

This extraordinary and barbaric game is played annually at Ashbourne and is almost without rules. The original rules simply barred murder and manslaughter but later rules had to be introduced banning play after midnight and making it illegal to transport the ball by vehicle. Apart from that, 'anything goes'. The ball has to be especially tough and is made of leather and filled with cork shavings rammed in tightly. To start the game, the ball is 'turned up', i.e. thrown into the crowd, usually by some celebrity. In 1928 the most distinguished of all to make the 'kick-off' or 'turn up' was H.R.H. The Prince of Wales, afterwards Edward VIII and Duke of Windsor. Since that day the game has adopted the prefix 'Royal'.

The V.I.P. is given luncheon at *The Green Man and Black's Head* and afterwards everyone assembles at Shaw Croft where the ball is 'turned up' after a rendering of the National Anthem. After that all Hell is let loose. The so-called teams consist of those who live north of Henmore Brook (the Upwards or 'Uppards') and those who live south of it (the Downwards or 'Down'rds'). The respective goals are at Sturton Mill and Clifton Mill and this ensures that players inevitably must plunge into Henmore Brook, which does not seem to damp anybody's ardour.

In the unlikely event of a goal being scored before 5 p.m., a new ball is turned up and play starts again. Scorers keep the ball they have scored with, so new ones are made each year.

It is a very rough game and affords a wonderful opportunity for the young people of the district to let off steam and display their aggressive instincts in a relatively harmless way.

HONOURING ROMAN CATHOLIC MARTYRS

In the first half of the 20th century there has been a great reconciliation between the Anglican Church and Rome. Old prejudices are dying quickly and there is more a feeling of Christian brotherhood rather than bigoted animosity. Yet, historically, both camps had their martyrs, particularly in the 16th century. In Derbyshire, on July 24th 1588, the year of the Armada, two Roman Catholic priests, Robert Ludlam and Nicholas Garlick, were found ministering to the needs of a famous recusant family, the Fitzherberts, at their grand house at Padley, near Grindleford. The unfortunate priests were taken to Derby and twelve days later suffered the terrible end of being hanged, drawn and quartered. The two Fitzherbert brothers who lived at Padley both died in prison. Padley passed from the family and fell into ruins.

The old family chapel remained but it was used as a barn and cow-house until 1932 when it was rescued by the Catholic Diocese of Nottingham. The old altar stone was found and reinstated and a year later the building was opened as a place of worship once again and Mass was celebrated openly for the first time since the Reformation. The building has become a place of pilgrimage to honour the two martyrs.

Each year on the Thursday nearest to July 20th pilgrims gather from far afield and process to the Chapel where a service is held.

PEELS, TOLLS AND CURFEWS

Curfews were bells rung at nightfall to indicate to travellers that a town or village was near and to warn them to come to safety. This long archaic practice survives in some parts of Derbyshire.

A curfew has been rung at Chapel-en-le-Frith since the 11th century but in addition there are morning bells followed by a toll indicating the day of the month.

At Matlock parish church the Angelus (commemorating the Incarnation) is rung at noon.

At Scarcliffe the Curfew Bell is rung for six weeks around Christmas, supposedly in memory of 'Lady Constantia' the name given to the effigy of a young woman in the church, probably a member of the de Frecheville family, with her infant. She obviously died in childbirth but legends have arisen around this remarkable piece of sculpture. It is said that the girl had an illegitimate child and later ran away with it. She got lost but the curfew guided her home safely with her baby. She left five acres of land to pay for the ringing of the curfew forever. The story hardly stands up on any counts, but the curfew continues.

THE WOODLANDS LOVEFEAST

King Charles II was too amiable a man to do much physical harm to anyone who offended against his type of religion. Early in his reign penalties were enacted against nonconformists (the King had pronounced that Presbyterianism was 'no religion for a gentleman') but such legislation did not stop people worshipping in the way they thought best, particularly in remote areas.

Thus nonconformist services were held in quiet places hidden from the mainstream of life. One such place was the tiny hamlet of Alport in the narrow valley of the river of the same name with the stone outcrop 'Alport Castles' rising on one side. The place chosen was an ordinary barn and it became famous as a place of Methodist worship, Wesley himself having preached here. For over three centuries the custom of holding nonconformist services has been kept up although there have been no laws against dissenters for generations. Inside, the barn has remained just a barn without a single symbol or object inside to associate it with religious rites. Yet on the first Sunday of July each year people assemble here in the morning. The floor is strewn with straw and a service takes place. Then in the afternoon follows the 'feast' consisting of pieces of fruitcake washed down with water.

OTHER CUSTOMS

Apart from those customs which are unique to the county, Derbyshire, like other counties, has ancient practices which have no special local significance, such as morris dancing and guisering (people dressing up, hence 'disguise') and kit-dressing ('kit' being the north country name for a pail or milk churn).

Many old customs have died out, such as the old ladies who were paid to dust the monument to Anthony Bradshaw in Duffield Church and the squirrel hunting in the same village. Are Thor Cakes still baked in Matlock on Guy Fawkes Night? Is posset still drunk on Christmas Eve? Do children still drop new pins in wells on Palm Sunday? And is there frumenty still for tea?

LEISURE ACTIVITIES IN DERBYSHIRE

The names and addresses of secretaries of the sporting clubs and associations referred to in this section can be obtained from The Reference Library, Derby City Library, The Wardwick, Derby (Tel: 2931111).

ARCHERY More than one type of archery is keenly practised in many parts of Derbyshire and there are several archers of national repute at present practising the sport in this county. Target Archery is under the governance of the Grand National Archery Society and the local Association is The Derbyshire County Archery Association. Field Archery (in field archery archers shoot at animal targets in undulating wooded countryside) comes under the auspices of the English Field Archery Association and there is a local Secretary in Nottinghamshire. The target archery bodies are affiliated to their international organisation, Féderation International de Tir a l'Arc (FITA) and the Field Archery Clubs to the International Field Archery Association for International Competition.

There are a dozen or more archery clubs in the county.

ATHLETICS The Indoor Sports Centre, Moor Lane, Derby, has facilities for squash, badminton, table tennis, indoor cricket, trampolining, weight-lifting, gymnastics, archery, shooting. The Municipal Athletics Stadium, also in Moor Lane, has a first class running track and athletics equipment. Other Sports Centres can be found in Alfreton, Belper, Chesterfield, Dronfield, Sandiacre and Staveley.

BADMINTON The Derbyshire Badminton Association consists of and represents over 70 clubs throughout the county. The Association organises Open, Restricted, Moderate and Junior Tournaments to provide competitive badminton for players of all standards and ages.

Two leagues operate within the Association for interclub competition. Both the Derby and District League and the North Derbyshire League have sections for men's, ladies', mixed and singles play.

Coaching is also organised with courses in different parts of the county using the services of 50 qualified coaches. These activities enable the D.B.A. to groom and sponsor the better players for the County Team.

BOWLS The county has both crown and flat green associations, adherents to the former predominating. There are abundant facilities for both resident and visitor at Buxton, Matlock, Derby, Chesterfield, Whaley Bridge, Alfreton, and other parts of the county.

CAVING AND POTHOLING Derbyshire and parts of adjacent Staffordshire provide unrivalled scope for caving and potholing but it cannot be emphasised enough that caving and potholing can be dangerous pursuits for the uninitiated. Anyone interested in taking up these pastimes is strongly advised to join a club. There are over 40 Derbyshire clubs in the Midlands and elsewhere which are affiliated to the Derbyshire Caving Association. The Hon. Sec. of the Association will offer advice on the subject if you telephone (0602) 821887.

CRICKET Derbyshire County Cricket Club was founded in 1870. Two thirds of its matches are played on the County Ground, Nottingham Road, Derby, now the Club's permanent home with a new pavilion, and a third at Queen's Park, Chesterfield. There are now annual fixtures at other grounds including Knypersley, Heanor and Leek. The team won the County Championship in 1936, the Nat. West Trophy in 1981, the Refuge Assurance League in 1990 and were runners-up in the Benson and Hedges Cup in 1988 and the Refuge Assurance Cup in 1990. The Club boasts some of the best players in the county. The pavilion may be hired for exhibitions and weddings. Details may be obtained from the Secretary, The County Ground, Nottingham Road, Derby. (Telephone: Derby 383211).

CRUISING In the southern parts of the county, mainly in the environs of Trent Lock and river stretches running from it and taking in the delightful canal stretches, there is a booming motor-cruiser season each year. From eight-berth cruisers down to camping cruisers (you travel by boat and camp on or near it at night) there is every kind of craft to be had. Most are privately owned, others are hired for periods upwards of a week. Many of the boats to be seen are built here (there are several good boat builders in this area) and many old narrow-boats have been converted for pleasure cruising. There are also many privately owned motor launches and outboard boats which use the water hereabouts for excellent weekend and summer holiday sport.

CYCLING Derbyshire has many byways suitable for cycling and there is no better county to explore in this way. Bicycles may be hired at Ashbourne (0335) 43156; Derwent (0433) 51261; Parsley Hay (0298) 84493; Waterhouses (0538) 308609; Middleton Top (0629) 823204; Hayfield (0663) 46222 and Shipley Country Park (0773) 719961.

FISHING Almost the whole of the fishable rivers and streams of Derbyshire are within the area of Severn-Trent Water Limited, whose licences are required prior to fishing. These are obtainable from many fishing tackle dealers and other various distributors in the area, or from the offices of the Area Fisheries Manager, Severn-Trent Water, at Meadow Lane, near Trent Bridge, Nottingham. The close season for brown and rainbow trout extends from 16th October to 17th March inclusive. The close

season for freshwater fish extends from 15th March to 15th June inclusive. The possession of a Trent area rod licence does not, of course, permit anyone to fish anywhere without, in addition, the consent of the riparian owner or tenant.

The Erewash, which forms the eastern borders of the county, the lower reaches of the Dove affected by the waters of the Staffordshire Churnet and the lower reaches of the Derwent were long ruined for fishermen by pollution but they are now considerably improved, particularly the Dove and Derwent. The Trent at Swarkestone, Willington and Shardlow, shunned for some time past by local anglers, has been fishing very well for quite some time now, but the lower part of the Amber contains only a few fish owing to poor water quality.

Trout fishing in the county attracts a considerable number of anglers. Both the Wye and the Derwent contain the coveted rainbow, and other notable trout streams in which perfect conditions prevail are the Dove (throughout the dales and for a considerable stretch below Ashbourne until the junction with the Churnet); the Manifold, Lathkill, Bentley Brook, upper Amber, Ecclesbourne, Bradford and Longford Brook.

Although the name suggests an anglers' rendezvous, the Izaak Walton Hotel at Dovedale welcomes others as well as exponents of fly-fishing. The Hotel, however, does control two miles of both banks of the Dove. Fishing is strictly reserved for hotel residents and is dry and wet fly only. A daily charge is made, but there is no fishing after 15th October.

The Charles Cotton Hotel, Hartington, reserves a section of the Dove for residents. Four rods per day are allowed to residents in the hotel. Day tickets are obtainable at Wetton Mill for a stretch farther downstream on the Manifold.

The Peacock Hotel, Rowsley, has over seven miles of fishing in the River Wye (said to be the only English river in which rainbow trout reproduces naturally) from Rowsley to near Ashford which is for dry fly only. Fishing rights are reserved for residents at a daily charge.

Season and day permits for the Ladybower reservoir (fly fishing only) are available solely from the Bamford office. Supplementary permits are available for juveniles under eighteen years who are accompanied by an adult permit holder. Prices on application. Fishing boats can be hired from the Fishery Office (0433) 51254. The season opens in Spring and closes on 13th October. Anglers over twelve must hold a current Severn Trent rod licence.

Day permits for Ogston reservoir (fly fishing only) may be obtained from the New Napoleon Inn, Woolley Moor, Ogston, or in advance from the Matlock office of the Severn Trent Water Limited. Supplementary permits for juveniles (12 to 17 years) are available. Prices on application. The reservoir is stocked before the opening of the season which is from 1st April to 15th October. Anglers over twelve must hold a current Severn Trent rod licence.

Season permits for the Linacre reservoir (fly fishing only) are available from the Matlock office of the Severn Trent Water Limited (0629) 55051. Day permits may be obtained in advance from the Matlock office or the Keeper's house at the reservoir. Supplementary permits are available for juveniles under eighteen years who are accompanied by an adult permit holder. Prices on application. The reservoir is stocked at intervals throughout the season which opens on the 1st April and closes on 30th September. Anglers over fourteen years must hold a current Yorkshire Water rod licence.

The Matlocks Angling Club controls a substantial amount of waters in the area, both for coarse and trout fishing and has a small but thriving match-fishing section. In addition, the Club also caters for junior members up to the age of 16 years.

Day permits are available for a limited number of waters in the Matlock town centre and Matlock Bath areas. The permits can be obtained from Vickers Newsagents, Bank Road, Matlock, and Bob Price, Newsagent, South Parade, Matlock Bath.

It is necessary to be in possession of a Severn Trent Water Limited rod licence before fishing these waters.

The main species of fish in the river at Matlock and Matlock Bath are trout and grayling. In addition there are some minor species such as chub, dace, roach and barbel.

The Derby Angling Association rent or own 14 miles of the Trent and Mersey Canal between Great Wilne and Clay Mills, and ten miles of almost all of both banks of the River Trent between Swarkestone and Willington, one mile of the River Mease at Alrewas, Anchor Church Pools, Swarkestone Gravel Pit, Wanlip Sailing and Marina lakes and part of the River Soar at Wanlip.

The Derby Railway Institute Fishing Club has the fishing rights in the River Trent from above King's Mills; Weston-on-Trent, to a point beyond the Cavendish Bridge; Shardlow, both sides of the river; Barrow-on-Trent; the canal in the parish of Weston-on-Trent and various ponds at Barton and Walton, Long Eaton and Sawley and near Willington. The club also has fishing rights in the River Dove at Tutbury. All this is included in the coarse fishing season ticket. Anyone fishing on these waters, however, must hold a Severn-Trent rod licence. Trout and grayling fishing is available in the River Derwent from Cawdor railway bridge to Darley Bridge, where three sections are reserved for fly fishing. There is also fly fishing in the upper reaches of the Ecclesbourne but there are only a limited number of tickets available. In addition, approximately one mile of Sutton Brook is available to holders of this ticket with special permit. No day tickets.

Coarse fishing is available to the public in the grounds of Kedleston Hall: in the Island Water above the Adam Bridge and the two lakes below from 16th June except Tuesdays and Fridays. Tickets are available at the North Lodge and the hours of fishing are from 8.30 a.m. until 7 p.m. until the end of September and thereafter until 5 p.m.

Good sport is available on the Derwent between Milford and Little Eaton including the low reaches of the River Ecclesbourne. These waters are under the control of the Derbyshire Angling Federation, which re-stocks annually with trout and coarse fish. Their season and day-tickets are available at the Bridge Inn, Duffield.

Fishing in the lakes at Allestree (bottom lake only), Markeaton and Alvaston Parks and on the Derwent at Darley Abbey and Ban's Wreck for carp, tench, bream and roach. Multi-site tickets available from the park rangers. Enquiries to Leisure Services Dept., Council House, Derby. (telephone 255919).

FOOTBALL Derby County, who are in the First Division, can be seen at the Baseball Ground on alternate Saturdays during the football season. Tel: 40105.

Chesterfield are in the Fourth Division, with fixtures at home on alternate Saturdays.

GLIDING During every weekend of the year, the graceful sport of gliding and soaring may be watched at Camphill on the moors above Great Hucklow, Derbyshire, in the Peak District. Spectators are

A glider at Great Hucklow

admitted to the Viewing Enclosure; a public car park and amenities are provided.

The Derbyshire and Lancashire Gliding Club was founded in 1934 and established in one of the picturesque old Derbyshire farmhouses, perched on an escarpment between Great Hucklow and Abney. It has a flying field of over 90 acres from which it operates some 30 Club and private aircraft. Camphill was the scene of many pre- and post-war National Gliding Competitions and the World Gliding Championships were held there in 1954.

During the summer months, the Club runs a series of holiday courses for members of the public wishing to sample the sport. The courses lasts for 5 days and course members are accommodated in the clubhouse, where full board is provided. Dual-controlled two-seater gliders are used for instruction, which continues from Monday to Friday. Details of vacancies and prices are available from The Steward, The Gliding Club, Camphill, Great Hucklow, Buxton, Derbyshire (0298 871270).

GOLF The only 18-hole course in Derby at present is that laid out by the Corporation at Sinfin; but the attractive Chevin course, near Duffield, and those at Allestree and Mickleover, and in the magnificent-timbered park at Kedleston Hall are within easy reach; the well-known Erewash Valley course at Stanton-by-Dale is but a little farther afield.

Buxton still has the Buxton and High Peak and the Cavendish clubs – both exceptional and with magnificent scenic backgrounds. Not far to the North are the popular lay-outs at Chapel-en-le-Frith and Matlock. Horsley Lodge (18 holes, par 72) is 6,300 yards long and near Horsley village. It has a residential, licensed club house.

A particularly well-kept and testing course is that of the Burton Golf Club on high ground at Bretby.

The Chesterfield Municipal course at Tapton is extremely popular while the course of the Chesterfield Club at Walton is well supported and a fine test of golf. Farther to the South-East lies the Ormonde Fields Club, near Codnor.

The Sickleholme Club at Bamford, although not a member of the Derbyshire Union, has its interesting and attractive course in the Hope Valley, part of the Peak National Park.

Breadsall Priory Club and course lie close to Derby and adjacent to the Breadsall Priory Hotel.

There is an eighteen hole golf club at Shirland, the Shirland Golf and Squash Club.

The nine-hole courses of the county are full of interest and well worth visiting. They are especially noteworthy for their individuality, variety of terrain, and some fascinating golf holes.

Courses available are: 18 holes; Allestree Municipal (near Derby), Burton (Bretby), Buxton and High Peak, Cavendish (Buxton), Chapel-en-le-Frith, Chesterfield Municipal (Tapton), Chesterfield (Walton), Chevin (Duffield), Derby Municipal (Sinfin), Erewash Valley (Stanton-by-Dale), Horsley, Kedleston Park, Matlock, Mickleover (near Derby), Ormonde Fields (Codnor), Sickleholme (Bamford). Nine-holes: Alfreton, Clifton (Ashbourne), Bakewell, Glossop and District, Ilkeston Borough, New Mills and Stanedge (Chesterfield).

GROUSE SHOOTING AND ACCESS AGREEMENTS

Large parts of Kinder, Bleaklow and the North Longdendale moors are open to the public through access agreements between the owners and the Peak National Park authority, except when grouse shooting is taking place. During the season, between 12th August and 10th December, some moors are closed for up to fourteen days: dates are listed on notices around the area. Particularly in August, September and October, the public should plan their routes carefully to avoid moors which are closed. Public rights of way are not affected. There is no shooting on Sundays but at this time of year there are quite a few closures on Saturdays.

It is important to note that the above applies to those moors where access agreements exist, and that on these moors the public must observe a few simple rules in exchange for access on over 350 days each year; for instance, that dogs must be on a lead. There are other moors where there is no public right of access at any time. For lists of shooting dates, maps showing access areas and other information write to the Peak National Park Office, Baslow Road, Bakewell, enclosing stamped addressed envelope.

HUNTING

The Meynell and South Staffordshire Foxhound hunts, which are both old established packs, amalgamated in May, 1970, forming one hunt known as the Meynell and South Staffordshire Hunt. The country covers the same as that previously hunted independently – south Staffordshire and south Derbyshire. Much of the terrain is still grassland and remains one of the finest hunting countries in England.

During the hunting season hounds meet on Tuesdays, Thursdays and Saturdays. Further details may be obtained from the Hunt secretaries: Mr. and Mrs. P. King, North Farm, Brailsford, Derbyshire.

The Barlow Foxhounds hunt the county to the east of the River Derwent including all of the county to the north-east, and southwards to Ambergate. The Secretary of the Barlow Hunt Supporters' Club will give locations of the meets and any other information.

Derbyshire hunting country

Derbyshire has a celebrated pack of harriers, the High Peak, which hunts the long-legged mountain hare over stone-wall country calling for intrepid horsemanship. Much of this area is over 1,000 feet above sea level. The pack hunts two days a week throughout the season (Wednesdays and Saturdays) and a point-to-point meeting on Easter Tuesday is held on Flagg Moor every year. The best centres for anyone wishing to hunt are Bakewell and Buxton and sport during past seasons has been good.

RAMBLING

The Derbyshire Area of the The Ramblers' Association is concerned with fostering a greater knowledge, love and care of the countryside, the preservation of natural beauty and the protection of footpaths.

Rambles, footpath walks and footpath surveys are arranged on Saturdays and Sundays throughout the year and on midweek evenings during the summer months from Derby, Belper, Matlock and Bakewell. During winter months talks/film evenings on matters associated with the aims of the RA are held.

The Area is affiliated to the Council for the Protection of Rural England through the two local branches, and with the Derbyshire Footpaths Preservation Society and the Park and Northern Footpaths Society, and works closely with these organisations.

The Derby Nomads, CHA/HF Rambling Club, Long Eaton Rambling Club and the Alfreton Rambling Club are all affiliated to the RA.

The footpath warden scheme whereby a member looks after the footpaths in a particular parish, and projects for footpath clearing and waymarking, give opportunities for members who do not necessarily wish to participate in the rambles.

Programmes and further information can be obtained from the Area Secretary and Group Secretaries. *All ramblers should note that walking over the moors is restricted during the grouse shooting season – see under* GROUSE SHOOTING.

RIDING

Derbyshire has some wonderful country for hacking and trekking and there are a number of excellent establishments offering expert tuition throughout the county.

Alton Riding School, Alton, Chesterfield, Derbyshire. S42 6AW. Tel: (0246) 590267.

Belper Riding Centre, Whitehouse Farm, Belper Lane, Belper, Derbyshire. DE5 2UJ. Tel: (077 382) 4080.

Birchwood Riding Centre, 140 Birchwood Lane, Somercotes, Derbyshire, DE55 4NE. Tel: (0773) 604305.

Brimington Equestrian Centre, 130 Manor Road, Brimington, Chesterfield, Derbyshire, S43 1NN. Tel: (0246) 235465/566132.

Buxton Riding School, Fern Farm, Fern Road, Buxton, Derbyshire, SK17 9NG. Tel: (0298) 72319.

Causeway Farm, Plaistow Green, Crich, Nr. Matlock, Derby. Tel: (0629) 534248.

The East Midlands Riding Association for Handicapped Children and Adults. Leathersley Lane, Scropton, Derby, DE6 5PN. Tel: Burton-on-Trent (0283) 812753.

Elvaston Castle Riding Centre, Thulston, Derby, Derbyshire, DE7 3EP. Tel: Derby (0332) 751927 or 753481.

Field Farm Stables, The Field, Shipley, Nr. Heanor, Derbyshire, DE7 7JH. Tel: (0773) 713164.

Hargate Hill Riding School, Hargate Hill, Glossop, Derbyshire, SK13 9JL. Tel: (04574) 65518.

Markeaton Riding Centre and Stud Markeaton Lane, Markeaton, Derby, DE3 4NH. Tel: Derby (0332) 40126.

Morley Riding Stables, Lime Lane, Morley. Tel: (0332) 831584.

Northfield Farm Riding and Trekking Centre, Northfield Farm, Flash, Quarnford, Nr. Buxton, Derbyshire. Tel: Buxton (0298) 22543.

Parkside Riding Stables, Wingfield Road, Alfreton. Tel: (0773) 835193.

Red House Stables, Old Road, Darley Dale, Matlock, Derbyshire, DE4 2ER. Tel: Matlock (0629) 733583.

Stubley Hollow Riding Centre, Stubley Hollow, Dronfield, Woodhouse, Nr. Sheffield, South Yorkshire. Tel: Dronfield (0246) 419207.

Whitehouse Farm Stables, Morley Lane, Stanley, Derbyshire, DE7 6EZ. Tel: Ilkeston (0602) 324142.

Yew Tree Farm Stables, Hazelwood, Derbyshire, DE6 4AE. Tel: Derby (0332) 841364.

Mention should also be made of the Derbyshire Horse and Pony Society – formed some years ago to look after the interests of all who ride or are concerned with horses. Particular emphasis is made on the retention of bridleways.

Within the White Peak area of the Peak National Park there is a network of waymarked routes for riding.

ROCK CLIMBING Although the Lake District and Wales have rock climbs whose height is greater than those of the Derbyshire crags, this area is unique in the scope it offers to the rock climber. The North and East of the county contain the Millstone Grit edges which provide climbs of every standard suitable for the complete beginner or the expert. Birchen's Edge and Gardom's Edge above Baslow and Windgather Rocks near Whaley Bridge are usually thought to offer climbs more suitable for the less experienced. The many buttresses of Kinder Scout; Froggatt and Curbar Edges above the village of

Curbar hold climbs which will tax even the best climber. These edges are of completely 'free' climbs. Millstone Edge near the Surprise View has, besides its many 'free' routes, some artificial climbing for which much artificial aid is needed. The use of these pitons, wedges, golos, mollys, fifis, etriers and other equipment is extremely complicated and a great deal of experience is needed.

The South and West of the county contain the Limestone Edges. There is a small area of Dolomite (Magnesian Limestone) near Brassington which offers climbing unique in this country. Although short, these pinnacles are very steep with pock holes giving amazing holds. More than any other rock in the county this rock is easily worn away and nailed footwear should never be used on any of the climbs or future generations will have no climbing to enjoy. The major attraction of this area is, however, the wealth of steep, hard climbing on the carboniferous limestone of the dales of the White Peak. Stoney Middleton; the Wye banks between Buxton and Monsal Dale (Cheedale, Miller's Dale, and Water-cum-Jolly); High Tor, Willersley; Wildcat near Matlock; the towers and pinnacles of the Dove; these form a climbing Mecca unsurpassed in England. The crags are steep, most of the routes are very hard and are certainly not for the inexperienced.

Derbyshire County Council has its own 'Outdoor Pursuits Centre' at White Hall, Buxton, where courses on rock climbing and kindred activities are given to young people, who need not be Derbyshire residents. Hollowford Training and Conference Centre, Hollowford, Castleton, also runs courses of the same type. Applications should be made to the Principal in each case.

Rock climbing is an exciting, worthwhile, but dangerous sport. No beginner should start without guidance from an experienced climber. If the beginner is not able to attend one of these centres he should contact a recognised climbing club. A full list of the clubs operating in the Peak District may be obtained from the Secretary of the Peak Committee of the British Mountaineering Council (061 273 5835).

ROWING Derby has two clubs where facilities for men's and women's rowing are provided. The Derby and Derwent Rowing Clubs have two well-equipped boathouses situated side by side, just within the Darley Grove entrance to Darley Park. In addition to excellent rowing facilities, both clubs have very good social amenities. The stretch of the River Derwent used for training is approximately one mile long extending from St. Mary's Bridge. The two clubs hold a joint annual regatta which is held early in May over a thousand metre upstream course. Visitors, or those wanting to join, should contact the secretary of the appropriate club.

Other boating facilities exist at Derby (Parks Department), Matlock Bath, Belper and Repton. It is advisable to apply to the appropriate local authority.

RUGBY FOOTBALL There are 16 clubs affiliated to the Derbyshire Rugby Football Union, which are as follows: Amber Valley, Ashbourne, Buxton Police, Dronfield, Hope Valley, Ilkeston, Glossop, Long Eaton, Matlock College of Education,

Old Baileans (Matlock), Old Mannerians (Bakewell), Rolls Royce (Derby), Old Tuptonians, Belper RFC and Swans RFC.

The County Union runs a County Senior Team, Under 23 and Under 21 teams. There is also a Derbyshire Schoolboys Union for boys who have left school, or who are at school.

Individuals interested in Rugby Football are invited to apply for membership to the Derby Rugby Football Club to the Hon. Sec., Derby RFU, The Pavilion, Kedleston Road, Derby.

SAILING The popularity of sailing is well reflected in the growth of sailing clubs in Derbyshire. Besides

Yachting in the Goyt Valley reservoir

its rivers, the county has several reservoirs upon which sailing is permitted. Sailing in these instances is strictly confined to club members and the clubs are responsible for the proper use of the water. On the rivers, the use of the water is less controlled.

The Trent Valley offers excellent facilities for inland yachtsmen and has one of the oldest clubs in the country – established in 1886 – The Trent Valley Sailing Club. Enquiries regarding membership should be sent to the Hon. Secretary, Trent Valley Sailing Club, Trent Lock, Long Eaton. Tel: (0602) 732587. Classes of dinghy raced are National 12 ft, Merlin-Rocket, Fireball, Swordfish and Optimist (for children). Racing takes place at weekends from the end of March to the end of October each year. There is a resident steward and full catering is provided.

The Staunton Harold Sailing Club with its clubhouse on the bank of the Staunton Harold Reservoir, has accommodation for approximately 300 boats. Novices are very welcome and RYA courses are organised here. Visiting members of clubs affiliated to the RYA are offered full facilities by prior arrangement and club members may introduce visitors. Classes of boats sailed are Fireball, Pegasus, Enterprise, GP14, Laser, Mirror 10 and Optimist. Tel: (0332) 862067.

In the Peak District are two well-established clubs – Combs and Toddbrook. The Combs Sailing Club operates on the Combs Reservoir near Chapel-en-le-Frith and co-operates with local Sea Scouts. The Club sails YW GP14 dinghies. The Club also has a Menagerie Fleet for other classes of dinghies.

A dinghy sailing club operates on Errwood Reservoir in the Goyt Valley and has Class Fleets of Enterprises, GP 14s, Graduates, Lasers, Mirrors and Scorpions.

Burton Sailing Club, which sails on the Foremark Reservoir, has Merlin Rockets, N 12, OK, Mirror and Scorpion Fleets. Class races are held on Saturdays and Sundays from March until December. Also Wednesday evening races are held in the summer. There is a very active social scene with functions for both children and adults. Membership application forms may be obtained from the Club house or from the Secretary.

Another of the 'reservoir' clubs in Derbyshire is Ogston Sailing Club.

The reservoir is about 200 acres in area and beautifully situated. The main classes sailed are 505s, GP14s, Enterprises, Ospreys and Larks.

Racing takes place on Saturdays, Sundays and many Wednesday evenings from April to the end of October.

The Hon. Secretary will be pleased to send full information to anyone interested, whether experienced sailors or novices.

The Long Eaton Sailing Club is situated on the banks of the River Trent with approximately six miles of sailing water. It has, at present, sixty members, but could accommodate up to eighty.

Racing takes place every Sunday for fleets of Enterprise, Mirror 10, Laser and Handicapped, with Wednesday nights set aside for Handicap racing. A very successful 'Frost Bite' is organised annually during November and December.

The Derwent Sailing Club (Tel: 863220) formed in 1959 originally sailed on the River Derwent at Darley Abbey but moved to Swarkestone Gravel Pits in 1967. The club sails at present the following classes: Graduate, Scorpion, Lark, Fireball, Laser, Wineglass, also a mixed fleet of other boats.

SHOOTING Derbyshire is well known for its grouse moors and the Twelfth is still an important day in the county's sporting calendar. Partridge and pheasant are in good number; and there is any amount of rough shooting available in most parts of the shire. There are a number of rifle and clay-pigeon clubs.

Though just outside the county – at Clipstone Drive, Forest Town, Mansfield – the Cavendish Gun Club draws many shooters from Derbyshire. It is one of the best and oldest shooting grounds in the country and well-known for its benign despotism. In fact, it seems to be a worthy upholder of the motto of the British Field Sports Association that 'all are welcome afoot or awheel!'

The Derbyshire Rifle Association, has sections for Fullbore Rifle (Prone), Smallbore Rifle (Prone, Standing and Kneeling), Pistol (Fullbore and Smallbore) and Air Weapons (Pistols and Rifle). There are 30 clubs in the county affiliated to the Derbyshire Rifle Association and the National Smallbore Rifle Association. All four sections are active in Club, County and National Competitions (Postal) and Shoulder to Shoulder Meetings including the famous Bisley shoot where the sport reaches its greatest heights.

SKI-ING When the snow covers the Derbyshire hills, the Edale Valley becomes a miniature Switzerland. Every other rambler seems to be armed with an ice-axe, for there is good practice ice-climbing in the gullies of Kinder Scout and Bleaklow. Sports outfitters are now supplying equipment to hundreds of new enthusiasts each season.

The slopes of nearby Rushup Edge, and the more gentle inclines around Buxton provide excellent training grounds for the novice, and fine glissades for the expert.

SWIMMING Derbyshire is well provided with swimming facilities, with indoor pools at Alfreton, Ashbourne, Belper, Bolsover, Buxton, Chesterfield, Clay Cross, Cresswell, Derby, Dronfield, Eckington, Etwall, Glossop, Heanor, Ilkeston, Long Eaton, Matlock, Ripley and Staveley. Outdoor pools can be found at Alfreton, Hathersage, Long Eaton, Staveley and Uttoxeter.

Some of the above mentioned pools are part of Leisure Centres which cater for a variety of sports including squash, badminton, gymnastics and other indoor ball games. These centres can be found in the county at the following places: Alfreton; Belper on the Kilburn Road; Chesterfield in Queen's Park; Derby on Moor Lane; Dronfield: and at Staveley.

TENNIS There are tennis clubs (about 60) in most districts of Derbyshire. Those at Ripley, with a floodlit court for winter play, and Duffield, with a squash court, being prominent in their own particular spheres. Derbyshire Lawn Tennis Association has its headquarters at Crewe Street, Derby and has a magnificent covered court. County matches, County championships, and other finals are staged here, and also much coaching is carried out in winter and summer.

Chesterfield, Belper, Netherseal and Alfreton are towns which provide very good facilities for tennis. Many of the large villages have a tennis club and details are to be found in the Derbyshire Lawn Tennis handbook obtainable from the Hon. Secretary. Tel: (0332) 766299.

TRAILING Of interest to ramblers, pony-trekkers and cyclists are the Tissington, High Peak, Monsal and the Sett Valley Trails. The Sett Valley Trail is the shortest trail being three miles long and it runs between Hayfield and New Mills.

The Tissington Trail set up by the Peak National Park is a scenic route 13 miles in length, running from

On the Tissington Trail

Ashbourne to Parsley Hay. The trail follows the old Buxton to Ashbourne railway line and the rambler or rider finds himself travelling through the matchless countryside of the National Park without the interference of cars, pollution and noise. There are car-parking facilities for people joining the trail at various stages. Walking and cycling routes, all clearly signposted, take the visitor to various local places of interest. There are also shorter routes for people who do not wish to wander too far: there are circular routes based on several of the car parks along the White Peak Scenic Route. At Hartington the old signal box is now an Information Point, open in summer on Saturdays, Sundays and Bank Holidays.

The High Peak Trail offers the same facilities and in fact joins up with the Tissington Trail at Parsley Hay, where there are toilet facilities for the disabled. The High Peak, however, is 17½ miles long and follows the old Cromford and High Peak Railway, starting at Cromford and finishing at Dowlow, south of Buxton.

Cyclists need not necessarily bring their own bikes as there is a hire service available between April and October. A returnable deposit is required and the cycles for hire can be found at the Parsley Hay car park (just off the A.515 approximately twelve miles from Ashbourne), at Middleton Top and at Ashbourne at Mappleton Lane.

For those without cars or those who don't wish to bother with driving, there are bus services operating in the Park area with extras on summer weekends. A 'Peak Wayfarer' ticket is available. It is a day rover valid on most 'bus and train services in North West Derbyshire, Greater Manchester and North East Cheshire. Details can be obtained from the National Park Office, Aldern House, Baslow Road, Bakewell, or at any of the National Park Information Centres. Tel: (0629) 814321.

Leaflets giving details of cycle hire and routes for the walker and cyclist can be had from these centres.

DERBYSHIRE THROUGH THE CENTURIES

DERBYSHIRE AS AN entity emerged sometime in the early 10th century and its boundaries at the Domesday survey were not changed until almost the dawn of the present century. Thus Derbyshire did not exist as a county or administrative unit of any kind at the time when Man is first known to have inhabited the area round about 5000 BC, nor when the Beaker people settled in the Peak nearly three and a half millennia later. Arbor Low is Derbyshire's little Stonehenge and is a relic of Bronze Age technology erected for religious practices or scientific knowledge, or both.

Other waves of immigrants using more sophisticated tools made of iron came into the area and established themselves in hill forts such as Mam Tor. Such fortifications were necessary to protect the occupants from attacks from neighbouring clans and became of vital importance during the Claudian invasion of Britain and its aftermath.

The Romans arrived hereabouts some thirty years after the second invasion but this wild and inimical country was not to their liking. They established military posts here, but the poor wretches who had to man them must have felt like Russian dissidents banished to Siberia. The sophisticated world of Rome at this time is vividly conjured up in the witty, pithy and often scandalous epigrams of Martial. The contrast between the hot pavements of the City with sun-drenched hills around coupled with soft living and plenty of Falerian wine, with the freezing rocky wilds of a Derbyshire winter is not difficult to imagine and for a sybaritic Roman it must have been well-nigh unbearable.

It is not surprising that, apart from the military forts at Melandra, Little Chester and elsewhere and the inevitable Roman chariotway Ryknield Street to facilitate troop movements, there are few domestic remains and no known luxurious villas with their mosaic pavements and hypocausts. Yet the area had its attractions for the Romans in the material sense – Derbyshire lead and bluejohn objects found their way into far corners of the Empire and they revelled in the warm spring waters of Buxton – a slight breath of home.

In the mid-5th century, some forty years after the last Roman soldier had packed his impedimenta and

Arbor Low

tramped back to Italy, new ruthless invaders sailed up the Trent – the Anglo-Saxons. They soon put down roots and their settlements eventually grew into the modern villages we know today. They called the area Mercia and eventually made their capital at Repton. By the mid-7th century these immigrants were now part of the young English nation and were converted

The Saxon crypt at Repton

to Christianity. Repton and Lichfield were important religious centres and parish churches were being founded such as at Wirksworth where the first modest building was erected in 653.

In the 9th century strange-looking craft were seen labouring up the Trent. Their prows had carved dragons as figure-heads and the occupants were wild, bearded and bibulous and of terrible aspect. They were barbarian Danes, far less benevolent than the Romans or even the Anglo-Saxons. They arrived to pillage and plunder. Pagans, they destroyed visible manifestations of Christianity wherever they could. King Alfred manfully kept them at bay in the south of Britain, but could not help much in the north and Midlands. The Danes captured Repton and they began, like their predecessors, to settle down and become part of the emerging nation. This area became part of the Danelaw – that part of England

The Wirksworth Stone – coffin lid of about AD 800 depicting scenes from the life of Christ. It is one of the most important relics of its kind in England

The ruins of 14th century Codnor Castle

allotted to the Danes by treaties with King Alfred and his successors.

In the fullness of time the Danes were converted. They even produced one splendid Christian king – Cnut – who was of the calibre of his Anglo-Saxon predecessors Alfred and Edward the Elder.

When the last great invasion took place in 1066, Derby was a county and England a completely

The Saxon cross at Eyam. The cross head is a rare survival

Christian country. The Normans consolidated the laws and customs of Edward the Confessor and in the next century began to build more substantial structures in the form of both churches and castles. Few of the latter remain in Derbyshire. The huge fortresses at Melbourne and Duffield have almost completely disappeared, others like Codnor survive in fragments, but Peveril Castle at Castleton is the one which has

A vase made from solid Blue John

survived the ravages of time and man the best. The thirteenth century saw the building of great abbeys and monasteries throughout the land. The chancel arch of Dale Abbey is, perhaps, the most dramatic relic of this period for, here again, Derbyshire, unlike its neighbour Yorkshire, is not rich in abbatial remains.

One Romanesque relic of immense importance and beautifully intact is the great church at Melbourne. Of its period it must be one of the most impressive in England.

After the Norman period, farming slowly developed throughout the county with special importance attached to sheep and cattle. In fact Derbyshire evolved much in the same way as its neighbouring counties, the main differences affecting this evolution being the mountainous characteristics of some parts of the area and the extraordinary richness of the land in minerals and stone. Apart from gold, lead and silver there were rich veins of alabaster and Derbyshire alabaster can be found in the form of beautifully carved monuments in churches all over the Midlands. Derbyshire also gave to the world its own unique mineral – bluejohn or Blue John – examples of which have been found in Rome and Pompeii.

The 15th and 16th centuries saw a dramatic rise in the prosperity of the gentry. The many small manor houses which abound throughout Derbyshire have parts dating from these periods. Wingfield, long a ruin, is the greatest from the later period, Haddon from the earlier. Like Wingfield, Haddon, too, was unoccupied for several generations and thus both buildings escaped modernisation and improvements and the prevailing winds of architectural fashion.

A powerful magnate of the 16th century was George Talbot, 6th Earl of Shrewsbury. His role as guardian of Mary Queen of Scots brought fame to Derbyshire as his royal prisoner was kept at various of the Earl's houses including Chatsworth. Shrewsbury's second wife, Bess of Hardwick, is one of the county's best-known daughters and by her second husband, William Cavendish, had several children from whom most of the old Derbyshire families descend and indeed many noble families from further afield.

Industrial development proceeded in the 17th century, harbinger of the Industrial Revolution which was soon to come. Thomas and John Lombe started a silk mill in Derby in the early years of the 18th century but it was not until people like Strutt and Arkwright put their ideas into practice that the Industrial Revolution really got under way and changed the face of England. They were followed by people like Brindley the canal builder and Stephenson the railway king, both with strong Derbyshire connections.

When the railways came to Derby in 1838 a new era opened. Derby was to become *the* railway town. Its magnificent station, started in that year and improved later in the century, was one of England's masterpieces of railway architecture. It was demolished, but the Midland Hotel (the first railway hotel), and the railway cottages, also the earliest of their kind, have been restored.

Restored railway cottages in Derby

The making of fine porcelain in Derby dates from the 18th century and Crown Derby is one of the country's most prestigious products about which so much has been written. Likewise with Rolls-Royce which came to Derby in 1908 and which made the county town famous throughout the world.

Further prosperity came to Derby with the advent of the Japanese Toyota motor-car company which is now established outside the City at Burnaston. Another major money spinner for the county is tourism. People began to come to see the wonders of

Three Famous Women connected with Derbyshire

Left: Elizabeth Hardwick, Countess of Shrewsbury

Right: Mary Queen of Scots, from the portrait at Hardwick

Far right: Lady Arbella Stuart, Bess of Hardwick's granddaughter

the Peak from early times, but it was not until the 18th century that this began to happen on any sort of scale. By the 1880s tourists were flocking to places like Matlock Bath, Buxton and Castleton, not only to see the sights, but also to take the health-giving water in the two former places. The sight of streets thronged with sightseers is nothing new. Today people come from all over the world visiting some of the great houses from the 15th to the 18th centuries such as Haddon, Hardwick, Chatsworth, Kedleston and Sudbury Hall. They explore the fantastic cave systems at Castleton and Matlock Bath and admire the mountainous, rugged countryside of the Peak District National Park.

In 1927 the old Parish Church of All Saints in Derby achieved cathedral status when Derby was made into a diocese of its own but it was not until 1977 that the town acquired the status of City.

Thus we attempt to cover a score of centuries of Derbyshire's history in a few hundred words – an impossible task. To sum up, our county has been given by the good fortune of geological chance some scenes of natural beauty second to none in the land. Through their merit and hard work the sons of

Derbyshire have enriched the world far beyond the narrow confines of the Dove and the Trent and their contributions to the spheres of industry, literature

St. Michael's Court

and poetry, architecture and commerce have afforded incalculable benefits to the Commonwealth and Empire and far beyond.

Derby past – a street scene of the 1860s

Derby present – the new Court House

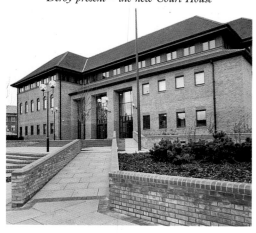

DERBYSHIRE A–Z

ABBOTSHOLME – See under Rocester

ABNEY *Map D.4*
A TINY hamlet set in lonely moorland country with wonderful views. Abney Grange, once the property of the Abbot of Welbeck, stands at the head of the beautiful gorge of Abney Clough, leading down towards Hathersage. Nearby are Abney Moor and the battlemented manor house of Highlow Hall.

ALDERWASLEY *Map H.6*
A PICTURESQUE hamlet on the hills between the Derwent and Ecclesbourne valleys. The old chapel of the Hurt family has recently been restored and has some sixteenth-century features; the new church, built in 1850, stands in the grounds of Alderwasley Hall, a large Georgian house with later additions formerly the principal seat of the Hurts but now a school. It faces across the beautiful wooded Derwent valley to Crich Stand. The name is pronounced 'Allersley'.

ALDWARK *Map H.5*
A HILLSIDE village close to the Griffe Grange Valley. Traces of a Roman road and the winding route of the Cromford and High Peak Railway are nearby. To the east is Ivonbrook Grange, a parish also known as Grangemill.

ALFRETON *Map H.8*
WITHIN EASY reach of some of Derbyshire's most attractive scenery, Alfreton is an industrial town on the A61 Derby-Sheffield road.
It was mentioned in the Domesday survey as 'Elstretune' and was a manor of some importance when Wulfric gave it to Burton Abbey towards the end of the Saxon era. After the Conquest, it came into the possession of Robert FitzRanulph, Lord of Alfreton, who founded Beauchief Abbey as a monastery of White Canons in the twelfth century. Later the manor was held by Ingram of Alfreton, then by the Chaworth family and subsequently by Sir Anthony Babington, of Dethick, whose grandson, Anthony, was executed in 1586 for his adherence to Mary Queen of Scots. The Morewoods became lords of the manor in 1629. Market rights were granted to Alfreton on 16th July, 1252.
Alfreton Hall, a stone mansion of 1750, was the seat of the Palmer-Morewood family until 1963 when the Hall and Park were acquired by the County Council and local Council. The Hall was partially demolished and the remainder has been converted into an Adult Education and Arts Association Centre and the Park is open to the public. Here is held the annual Roger Coke Memorial Concert (*vide* Pinxton).
There is a Lido in Alfreton Park with a separate diving pool, competition size swimming pool and children's pool, which is linked to a separate covered pool. Facilities for other sports are provided in the adjacent Leisure Centre.
The large parish church of St. Martin, near the entrance to the hall, has fourteenth-century nave arcades, an early fifteenth-century tower with a thirteenth-century tower arch (the oldest part of the building) and a fifteenth-century vaulted vestry, but the east end was rebuilt and other alterations made between 1869 and 1900. In the north aisle is the remarkably good monument to George Morewood (d. 1792).
The south end of the town was considerably improved by the generosity of Robert Watchorn, a pit boy who emigrated to America, made his fortune and returned to build the Robert Watchorn Memorial Church and a school.
Several interesting old houses survive in the town. The former George Hotel (now closed down), facing down broad King Street, is in fact a Georgian house, and at the corner of Church Street, close by, is an early eighteenth-century stone house. In King Street is a curious survival – the parish lock-up built about 1820, and in High Street, running east from the George Hotel, is an Elizabethan house with a three-storey porch.
To promote industry and provide employment, one site at Cotes Park has been developed and all the land on the former Alfreton Colliery site has been taken up. Further industrial land adjoining the Cotes Park site has been purchased by Derbyshire County Council.
The Alfreton by-pass road (A38) meets the M1 at intersection 28 and places the town in a favourable position for easy access.

ALKMONTON *Map L.4*
NOTHING REMAINS of the old village except bumps in the ground. These, however, show clearly the lines of streets and the sites of cottages. The present Alkmonton is about a mile to the north of its original site, and the only object in common is the Norman font in the church. (Cf. Hungry Bentley).

ALLESTREE *See under Derby*

ALPORT *Map H.5*
A QUIET village with some fine old houses near Youlgreave and Rowsley where Bradford Brook joins the Lathkill though once it was a lead-mining centre. Not far off is Harthill Hall, a former seat of the Cockayne family.

ALPORT HEIGHT *Map H.6*
ONE OF the highest points of the Low Peak (1,034 ft), this hill-top of nine acres, between Wirksworth and Ambergate, was presented to the National Trust in 1930 by an anonymous donor and commands very fine views over a wide area. A massive gritstone monolith (Alport Stone) has been popular with rock climbers and an old stone direction sign, rescued from duty as a gate-post, has been re-erected here. It points the way to 'Ash-born', 'Darby', and 'Wirksworth', and is dated 1710. The summit of the Height is crowned by the aerials of the Derbyshire County Police. Here, in 1977 and again in 1981, bonfires were lit in the national chain of bonfires to celebrate Queen

Waterfall at Alport, near Youlgreave

Elizabeth II's Silver Jubilee and the marriage of H.R.H. the Prince of Wales.

ALPORT MOOR *Map B.3*

THIS VAST moorland area rises to a height of 1,760 feet and adjoins Bleaklow Hill (2,060 ft). The river Alport has its source here and meanders through a panoramic valley. This is one of the loneliest places in the county and one of great beauty. 'Alport Castle' is a dramatic outcrop of rock.

ALSOP-EN-LE-DALE *Map H.4*

THIS SMALL village is situated near the River Dove. Its Norman Church of St. Michael and All Angels, formerly a dependency of the church of Ashbourne, has complete registers from 1701. The most interesting features are the Norman doorway on the south side, the head of which has a double chevron moulding, and a Norman window that still remains in the south wall. The building consists of chancel, nave 32 feet long and western tower, and in view of its size another point of interest may be found in its walls which are unusually massive for such a building, being about three feet thick throughout. The old stone corbels of the earlier roof can still be seen in the nave. There is a pretty Elizabethan hall nearby.

ALVASTON AND BOULTON *See under Derby*

AMBERGATE *Map H.7*

HERE THE River Amber joins the Derwent close to

41

the main A6 road to the Peak. Alport Height lies a few miles to the west and other beauty spots and places of interest make this an ideal point for starting cross country rambles. There is a late Victorian church but Francis Thompson's station of 1840 has gone. See also South Wingfield.

ARBOR LOW *Map G.4*

THIS FINE stone circle is to be found on the hills near Youlgreave and Monyash and is under the control of English Heritage. Access involves traversing private land for which a charge is levied. Though the stones are in a recumbent position, the main circle is 812 feet in circumference, enclosed by a ditch. Connected to it by a continuous earth bank is a sepulchral mound known as Gib Hill. Excavations have revealed Bronze

Age remains. It is one of the many mysterious stone circles to be found throughout Britain. An arrow-head found there dates back to 1800 BC. Many other earthworks and barrows are to be found on the surrounding hills. There are some exceptionally fine views to be had thereabouts of typical upland country. See p. 36.

ARLESTON

A DESERTED village site on the south edge of the Derby suburbs graced by a fine timber-framed house overlooking the canal and a near-by moated site.

ASHBOURNE *Map J.4*

THERE ARE parts of this pleasant market town which would still be familiar to Dr. Johnson and James

Ashbourne Church and gates

St. John Street, the town's main thoroughfare

Boswell were they to return from the dead for a day. The place lies at the southern end of the Peak District and is the gateway to Dovedale and the Izaak Walton country.

At one end of the main street stands the church of St. Oswald, described by George Eliot as 'the finest mere parish church in the kingdom'. It is a magnificent cruciform building with a 212 foot-high spire. Mostly of the early English style, the greater part was built in 1241. The chancel, built about 1220, is the oldest portion of the fabric and contains twelve lancet windows and the canopied tomb of Robert de Kniveton (d. 1471). Over the altar is a window by Kempe showing the arms of Normandy and England and France and England. Fine examples of stained glass can be seen throughout the church. The Boothby Chapel contains monuments of great interest, the most charming being the one in Carrara marble by Thomas Banks of Penelope Boothby who died in 1791 when only five years old. In St. Oswald's Chapel are three cannon balls which are said to have been fired at the church by Parliamentary troops.

The old Tudor building which stands near to the church was once the home of the Queen Elizabeth Grammar School. It was founded in 1585 by Sir Thomas Cockayne whose arms formed the school badge. Beside and opposite are two handsome houses designed by Joseph Pickford of Derby: the Grey House and The Mansion (see page 44). The school is now comprehensive and was transferred some time ago to a more modern building on the north-east side of town.

The annual Shrovetide football game, held on Shrove Tuesday and Ash Wednesday, attracts big

43

Grey House in Church Street

Ashbourne's famous Gingerbread House

crowds every year. The rival teams are hundreds strong. See page 28.

Opposite the old school is The Mansion, an early eighteenth-century house once occupied by Dr. John Taylor who was visited frequently by Dr. Johnson between 1737 and 1784, and nearby are the almshouses which are well worth a visit. Dr. Johnson would certainly be surprised to see an Indian restaurant and some of the fine and prestigious shops and shopping areas which add to the amenities of the town.

The surrounding district is essentially agricultural but there are a number of traditional industries in the town – milk and coffee products, knitwear, women's foundation garments and light engineering. Recently,

a modern industrial estate opened by the Council has attracted new and varied industries.

The town's amenities include beautiful walks, memorial gardens and playing fields with facilities for tennis, bowls, cricket, hockey, football, swimming and fishing.

The remaining portion of Ashbourne Hall, once the seat of the Cockayne family, is now used as the Public Library and partly as offices. Prince Charles Edward Stuart stayed a night here on his march to Derby in 1745 and also one night during the retreat.

The town centre forms part of a large Conservation Area in view of its buildings of historic and architectural importance, and in one of these buildings, No. 13 Market Place, a most attractive Tourist Infor-

The Sheepwash Bridge over the Wye at Ashford-in-the-Water

mation Centre has been established by the council. Further details about Ashbourne, Dovedale and the Peak Park can be obtained by telephoning Ashbourne 43666.

ASHFORD-IN-THE-WATER *Map E.4*

A PICTURESQUE village on the Wye 1½ miles north-west of Bakewell and 1 mile from Great Longstone. The curfew bell no longer rings, but the ancient Sanctus Bell still tolls during Consecration in Holy Communion at the Parish Church. The church was rebuilt in 1870, incorporating in the south door the original Norman tympanum, showing a tree of life in the centre, with a hog and wolf facing it. In the north aisle are hung four paper garlands or 'virgin crants' (compare *Hamlet, v.i.*), carried at the funerals of betrothed maidens. On the south wall is a tablet to Henry Watson (d. 1780) who in 1748 founded a black marble works. Inlaid Ashford marble became the principal industry of the village until early in the twentieth century.

The church's dedication is to the Holy Trinity and the Blessing of the Wells is the great event of the Patronal Festival – Trinity Sunday. The Sheepwash Bridge, close to the church, is one of several old bridges in or near the village. There are several fine houses in the locality, including Thornbridge Hall, a magnificent neo-Elizabethan mansion (now a conference centre) with stained glass windows by Sir E. Burne-Jones, fireplaces from Harlaxton Manor and Derwent Hall and Samuel Watson's 'Buffet Fountain' once at Chatsworth. On the surrounding hills are many prehistoric forts and burial mounds. Ashford Hall belongs to the Olivier family. Set in a pretty park, it was designed by Joseph Pickford in about 1770.

ASHLEYHAY *Map J.6*

ASHLEYHAY IS a minute but fascinating hamlet well off the main Derby to Wirksworth road. The church matches in size the tiny population.

ASHOVER *Map G.7*

AN OLD-WORLD village situated in the beautiful Amber Valley, 7 miles south-west of Chesterfield. Near the village are fine moorland country and rock formations, and many evidences of old-time mining may be found.

All Saints' Church, its graceful fifteenth-century spire, 128 ft high, a prominent landmark in the valley, has many relics of antiquity. The south door dates from 1275, the smaller north door from 1350. The fine alabaster tomb of Thomas Babington of Dethick was made in 1518, the rood screen, carrying the arms of Babington quartered with FitzHerbert, in 1511. The lead font, of about 1150, is ornamented with ten pairs of upright carved figures and is one of the few Norman lead fonts in England. The third bell of the peal, C sharp, bears the inscription 'The old bell rung the fall of Bonaparte and broke, April 1814'. The bell was re-cast in 1814 and again in 1890.

Eddlestowe Hall, now a farmhouse, situated to the right of the Matlock road as it ascends Slack Hill, was garrisoned by a troop of Royalist Dragoons in 1644. Eastwood Hall was destroyed by Parliamentarians after the defeat of the Royalists in 1646, but the ruins still stand. The early eighteenth-century Overton

Hall was once the home of Sir Joseph Banks, the celebrated naturalist. An agricultural show is held annually at Ashover in August.

The village centre of Ashover

ASHWOOD DALE *Map E.2.3*

ASHWOOD DALE is included in the parish of Kingsterndale. Lime kilns are relics of its past history.

ASTON *Map C.4*

ASTON HALL is very interesting to the architectural historian, says Pevsner, because of its date: 1578. The house, of two storeys, has five bays and a parapet rising in the middle into a steep gable. Roman Doric columns and a four-centred arch surround the doorway.

ASTON-ON-TRENT *Map M.8*

A LARGE village six miles south-east of Derby. All Saints' Church has a Norman west tower, late-thirteenth century nave and aisles, with a fifteenth century clerestory and a thirteenth-century font. The church possesses a rare bassoon used in the church orchestra before the universal introduction of organs. Aston Hall, a fine Georgian building, is now a hospital.

ATLOW *Map J.5*

A FARMING hamlet through which flows the pretty Henmore Brook on its way to Ashbourne. It has a pretty little Victorian Church, one of the last designs of the Derby architect H. I. Stevens.

AULT HUCKNALL *Map F.9*

A SCATTERED township, including Hardwick Hall and country park, Rowthorne, and Hardstoft (where oil was tapped some years ago). Four of the bells in St. John the Baptist's Church date from 1590. In the Hardwick chapel of the church is an unusual monument of 1627 to Anne Keighley, wife of the first Earl of Devonshire, and the tomb of the famous

Thomas Hobbes, the philosopher buried at Ault Hucknall

Below: The parish church of All Saints, Bakewell

philosopher, Thomas Hobbes, author of *The Leviathan*, who died at Hardwick in 1679. He was tutor to the second and third Earls of Devonshire and taught mathematics to the Prince of Wales (afterwards Charles II) who later became an expert in figures of another sort. The church has interesting examples of Norman and perhaps even earlier work. To visit Hardwick leave the M1 at junction 29 and proceed via Glapwell.

AXE EDGE *Map F.2*

FAMOUS as one of the finest panoramic view-points in Peakland, Axe Edge is traversed by the main road from Buxton to Leek. It offers a favourite motor run, and in almost all directions delightful walks abound. The high altitude (1,600 ft above sea level) provides a pure, crisp and bracing air. To the west, across the Cheshire border, is the Cat and Fiddle Inn, possibly the highest licensed house in England.

The River Dove, which is 45 miles long and drains an area of 95,000 acres, rises near the southern end of Axe Edge together with the rivers Wye and Dane.

BAKEWELL *Map F.5*

FROM THE quiet though prosperous country town of the 1940s, Bakewell has become the Piccadilly Circus of the Peak District complete with one-way streets. This is not to say that it has lost its appeal visually, but during the summer months it is often thronged with too many people for comfort.

Bad-kwell or bath-spring tells us why there has been a human settlement here since the Iron Age. The warm chalybeate-saturated waters from at least 12 wells have long-since been diverted to run into the Wye or have dried up, but they not unnaturally attracted the Romans as attested by the altar found hereabouts.

The earthwork now known as Castle Hill is said to have been a military post built by Alfred the Great's son Edward the Elder in 924 against the possibility of Danish attacks though historians now have some doubt about its nature.

The five-spanned Gothic arched bridge over the Wye in the centre of the town has been in daily use since about 1300. The large, handsome Georgian coaching inn, the Rutland Arms, proclaims one of the great families living near – the Manners, Dukes of Rutland of Haddon Hall, descendants in the female line from the Vernons of Haddon. Elsewhere in the town is *The Manners Arms* which, tactlessly, and for some unknown reason, displays the arms not of the Rutlands, but of the other ducal family, the Devonshires whose seat, Chatsworth, is also close by.

The fine spire of All Saints, the parish church, can be seen from most directions and the building stands on rising ground in a commanding position. There was a Saxon church here and many ancient fragments of stone remain to tell the tale including the shaft of an 8th century Anglian cross decorated with scrolls and scenes from the life of Our Lord. Most of the present building is 13th century though there was much restoration done by the Victorians. The church contains some superb monuments, especially the small wall monument of 1385 to Sir Godfrey Foljambe and his wife. In the Vernon Chapel are monuments to Sir George Vernon 'The King of the Peak' and to his daughter and co-heiress, Dorothy Vernon who married Sir John Manners and brought Haddon Hall to the family of the Dukes of Rutland.

Visit the old Market Hall. It is now the information centre for the Peak District National Park and here you should find all you need to know about the town and its surroundings (the headquarters of the Peak Park Planning Board is in Aldern House on the outskirts of the town). The Old House Museum gives marvellous glimpses into Bakewell's past. See page 4.

Agriculture is still Bakewell's basic activity and the Cattle Market is one of the largest in the county. The annual Bakewell Show, started in 1843, is the most important event in the town's calendar and one of the best agricultural events of its type in the country.

Richard Arkwright left his mark here when developing mills using water power. He built Lumford Cottages at Holme just outside the town.

The old Bakewell Pudding shop

Holme Hall is a very fine country house and near it is a famous packhorse bridge of about 1664.

The Lady Manners School was founded in 1637 as a grammar school but is now a comprehensive. S. Anselm's is a boys' preparatory boarding school.

All over the English speaking world the name of Bakewell is famous, for it is immortalised in the name of a certain type of sweetmeat. This is generally known as 'Bakewell tart' but more correctly 'Bakewell pudding'. Like Cooper's Oxford Marmalade it was the result of an accident in the kitchen. The result, instead of being thrown away, turned out to be extra delicious and the 'mistake' became a secret formula. The old Bakewell Pudding Shop is still a popular place in the town and the famous puddings can be bought here. Though there are many imitations, the original recipe is still a secret.

BALLIDON *Map H.4*

THIS TINY hamlet is easy to miss and Time itself seems to have left it high and dry. It is on a road to nowhere, near its larger neighbour Parwich. A certain amount of quarrying goes on around here but for the rest it is farming. If the village is easily missed, it is even easier to miss the sweet little Norman church (much restored) standing in a field away from the houses.

Remains of a larger medieval settlement are evident in the vicinity not to mention Bronze Age barrows and a fragment of Roman road.

BAMFORD *Map C.5*

THIS Derbyshire hill village, 12 miles west of Sheffield, is pleasantly situated on the eastern side of the Derwent. About a mile and a half north of the village begins the series of massive dams and great lakes forming the Derwent and Ladybower Reservoirs. Two villages, Derwent and Ashopton, now lie beneath the waters.

A magnificent run by car can be made from Bamford, along the fine road skirting the north shore of Ladybower Reservoir, thence over the Snake Pass to Glossop. Turning south, one proceeds via Hayfield to Chapel-en-le-Frith into Castleton, and through Hope to Bamford, Edale and the Hope Valley. Many other places of interest are within easy reach. There are fine bracing walks in several directions and an 18-hole golf course. Sheep-dog trials are held at Bamford every year and 'The Marquess of Granby' is a popular hostelry.

The church of St. John the Baptist and the vicarage have the distinction of being designed by William Butterfield, the architect of Rugby School Chapel and Keble College.

BARLBOROUGH *Map D.9*

THIS ANCIENT parish, 7 miles north-east of Chesterfield, has records dating from 1648. Barlborough Hall, an Elizabethan mansion built in 1583, was designed by Robert Smythson one of the famous family of mason-architects who lived not far away at Bolsover. It was originally the home of Francis de Rodes, who was one of the judges at the trial of Mary Queen of Scots. A characteristic example of the Elizabethan interpretation of Renaissance ideas, it is almost square in plan and is notable for its octagonal corner turrets, its decorative battlements and unusual steps to the raised terrace.

For the past two centuries the Grey Lady is reputed to have walked the corridors of the Hall, which is now a preparatory school for Mount St. Mary's College, Spinkhill. The schoolboys are not impressed by the

Barlborough Hall

ghostly heritage, yet old inhabitants of Barlborough tell of a daughter of the house who left for church on her wedding morn only to find that the bridegroom had met with a fatal accident when his coach overturned on the way to church. According to the legend the daughter returned home to the Hall and has been walking the corridors ever since looking for him. The entrance avenue to the Hall was planted during the reign of William and Mary. There are a number of interesting old houses in the village, including Barlborough Old Hall by John Smythson dating from 1617 and now restored.

BARLOW *Map E.7*
A TOWNSHIP on the fringe of the coalfield area, some 4 miles north-west of Chesterfield, possessing the small Norman Church of St. Lawrence, with registers dating from 1573. The triptych style of well-dressing is practised here; it began in 1840 as thanksgiving for the improved water supply when a village pump was installed. Flower heads, not petals, are used in the designs, and three wells are usually dressed. The

Barley or Barlow family originate from here, Robert Barley being Bess of Hardwick's first husband. Incised stone monuments to the family are in the church.

BARMOOR CLOUGH *Map D.3.*
TWO MILES from Chapel-en-le-Frith, to the right of Sparrowpit Road, is an ancient ebbing and flowing well. It seldom flows in a normal summer and never in a drought; but during a rainy period in mid-winter it works regularly, a flow occuring about every half-hour and lasting about five-minutes.

BARROW HILL *Map E.8*
TAKES its name from the Barrow family of Ringwood Hall, Chesterfield, who were Lords of the Manor of Brimington and for a century connected with Staveley Iron Works. The Church of St. Andrew was built in the 1890s in red brick. It has no tower but there is an interesting mosaic reredos.

BARROW-ON-TRENT *Map M.7*
THIS QUIET, unspoilt village between the River Trent and the Trent and Mersey Canal, lies about 6 miles south of Derby. The Church of St. Wilfred has Early English features, including the unusual piers of the north arcade, and a fourteenth-century tower, and contains a fourteenth-century alabaster effigy of a priest. The Hall burnt down in 1957 and modern housing now covers the site. George Turner painted landscapes in the area.

BASLOW *Map E.5*
ON THE edge of Chatsworth Park, Baslow is one of the most picturesque of Derbyshire villages, noted for its fine, ancient stone bridge of three arches over the Derwent, and for its magnificent position amid moorland and river scenery. The much-restored Church of St. Anne, on the Derwent banks, contains interesting monuments, and possesses a church dog

Cottages at Baslow near the entrance to Chatsworth Park

48

whip. Many curious stone slabs are to be found in the churchyard, together with stately elms and ancient yews. The church clock, installed to commemorate the Diamond Jubilee, has VICTORIA 1897 in place of numbers.

The Cavendish and *The Devonshire Arms* are two excellent places for refreshment. The former (once known as *The Peacock)* is an hotel with Chatsworth links. Thus the name was changed – a peacock being the crest of the Manners family, Dukes of Rutland. Today the knotted snake, the crest of the Cavendish family, Dukes of Devonshire, is in evidence.

Nether End, with its 'Goose Green', a triangular paddock with trees, is the popular meeting place of visitors to Baslow.

To the north lies the hamlet of Bubnell, unspoilt and having at its centre a seventeenth century hall.

BEELEY *Map F.5*

AN IDYLLIC gritstone estate village near the south end of Chatsworth Park. The Church of St. Anne, though practically rebuilt in 1884, retains a Norman doorway, a fourteenth-century tower, and several memorials to the Cavendish family. Registers date from 1538. Beeley Hall is of the early seventeenth century, but much of the house building was carried out at the time the sixth Duke of Devonshire was rebuilding near-by Edensor in 1839. The lovely old stone bridge over the Derwent near Beeley Lodge still provides the access to Chatsworth grounds on the Rowsley side. *The Devonshire Arms* is an excellent public house.

Beeley Moor (1,200 feet), rises above the village and feeds a stream into the Derwent in Beeley. Across stepping stones to the west bank, one climbs steep slopes to the thickly-clad Lindup woods.

The old inn has been modernised but still maintains its village character.

Hob Hurst's House is a prehistoric burial mound on Bunker's Hill, some 1½ miles north-east of Beeley and overlooking Chatsworth. Formerly a round barrow, it is the traditional home of Hob o'th'Hurst. Noble woods and green slopes of pastureland, chequered with lines and squares of hedgerows on the Chatsworth estate, indicate Beeley's ties with the ducal house of Cavendish.

BEESTON TOR *Map H.3*

THIS HUGE mass of limestone (Staffordshire) rises 200 ft from the river in the Manifold Valley, and is ¾-mile south of Thor's Cave, near the point where the Hamps joins the Manifold. At the foot of the rock is St. Bertram's Cave, where interesting prehistoric remains have been found.

BEIGHTON *Map C.8*

UNTIL 1967 in Derbyshire, Beighton is now in the City of Sheffield. It has an interesting church, St. Mary's, with unusual ornamented capitals, and a Georgian manor house in attractive farm surroundings.

BELPER *Map J.7*

GO TO Belper if you want to feel the last echoes of the Industrial Revolution. The attractive main street has two Georgian inns one of which has a Doric portico

which straddles the pavement. All around are surviving mills, the earliest dating from 1804.

The Strutt family, headed by Jedediah, developed the textile industry in the 18th century at Belper with new machinery. Unfortunately in recent years several of their original mills have been demolished but much still remains including a chapel and workers' houses built by the Strutts one of whom was eventually to be ennobled, taking the title of Lord Belper.

The name 'Belper' is a corruption of 'Beaurepaire' once a royal hunting ground. The place is mentioned in charters dated 1139 and 1272 and three parks stocked with deer existed at that time. The old church of St. John the Baptist is said to have been built by Edmund, Earl of Lancaster in the 1250s.

From the Strutts' time there has been a continuity of textile production with other mills dating from as late as 1912 and there are still some sewing-cotton and hosiery works.

Above: Belper Bridge and Strutt Mill, now a commercial complex

Jedediah Strutt by Wright of Derby

In spite of this long history of industrial development, it is still a pleasant country town with a distinctive atmosphere. There is even a certain cosmopolitan touch with a flourishing restaurant offering American regional food.

The river Derwent which flows through the town and once provided the Strutts with the power to drive their machinery offers opportunities for boating at the Belper River Gardens. The town has a large sports centre on Kilburn Road, and Belper Show is held annually on August Bank Holiday.

BERESFORD DALE *Map H.4*
REGARDED by many as the most beautiful of Peakland dales, the cliffs and rocks along Beresford Dale are curious in formation and there are several caves.

The Pike Pool in Beresford Dale

Below right: Bolsover's 'keep'

BIRCHOVER *Map G.5*
BIRCHOVER is set in the centre of magnificent rock scenery. The Rowtor Rocks, at the base of which is the *Druid Inn*, are a pile of gritstone about 70 yards in length, with several so-called rocking stones, including one of 50 tons. The Rev. Thomas Eyre (d. 1717) had some of the rocks here carved into seats. Robin Hood's Stride, with its two pinnacles, attracts the attention of rock climbers. Old stocks were restored to their original position at Upper Town in 1951. People of the Bronze Age buried the ashes of their dead in urns on near-by Stanton Moor and elsewhere in the district. Local relics of this period are now housed in Sheffield. A small hermitage concealed by a yew tree, at the base of the Cratcliffe Tors, contains a carved crucifix some four feet high, a niche for a lamp, and a seat hewn from the rock, all of which are of unknown antiquity.

BLACK ROCKS *Map H.6*
THE BLACK ROCKS, millstone grit outcrops on the hills between Cromford and Wirksworth, are certainly the most striking and conspicuous landmark in the district. The cliffs are some 80 feet high, and natural erosion has left five huge bastions of great beauty, all facing due north. These are in regular use by climbers. Near the foot of the Rocks there is a picnic area and car park adjacent to the High Peak Trail.

BLACKWELL *Map G.8*
FORMERLY an industrial and colliery parish in the upper Erewash Valley, with, in the old village itself, St. Werburgh's Church probably standing in a pre-Christian enclosure. A large fragment of an Anglian cross is preserved in the churchyard. The nave arcade of the church is ancient, with pre-Norman remnants. Jedediah Strutt (*vide* Belper) worked on his stocking frame at Newton Old Hall, now a farmhouse near the church.

BLEAKLOW *A.3*
A HIGH, uninhabited part of Peakland that provides good walking terrain for the hardy. Bleaklow is one of the biggest areas in England uncrossed by a road. Though, as its name suggests, bleak at times, in summer it is a place of great beauty.

BOLEHILL *Map H.6*
THIS ATTRACTIVE village clings to rising ground just a short walk to the north of Wirksworth and occupies several different levels. Its name proclaims its former importance as a lead-mining centre ('bole' being a cavity where lead was smelted). From here access is gained by foot to the top of Barrel Edge, the highest point around with magnificent views towards Matlock.

BOLSOVER *Map E.9*
THE FIRST glimpse of Bolsover and its castle approached from Chesterfield is a sight never to be forgotten. The waste-lands, chimneys and other relics of heavy industry and mining and the Victorian artisans' dwellings huddled in serried lines make an exciting and contrasting frame for the extraordinary castle perched on its hill with wooded and steeply sloping ground in front.

You will not find anything like this anywhere else in Britain. Although the site was once occupied by a Norman structure, the present building is a fantasy of 17th century baroque, much of it in ruins, and the work of members of the Smythson family of architects.

The building bug of Bess of Hardwick passed to several of her descendants, not least to her son, Sir Charles Cavendish, who started building the present Castle after acquiring it from his step-brother the 7th Earl of Shrewsbury in 1613, and Sir Charles's son, William, 1st Duke of Newcastle who was responsible for the riding school (he also built one at his other seat, Welbeck Abbey). Today the Riding School has been restored and is in use again for the disabled. There is an annual show here.

Black Rocks between Cromford and Wirksworth

Parts of this great palace were built to accommodate Charles I and his Queen when they stayed with the Cavendish family in 1634 and a special masque was written by Ben Jonson and performed in the Long Gallery in front of Their Majesties. It was called 'Love's Welcome at Bolsover'.

The 'keep' is the only habitable part remaining and is full of surprises. There are extraordinary and elaborate fireplaces and numerous somewhat crude murals in many of the rooms. Below are vast kitchens and cellars. From the roof wide panoramas of the Derbyshire countryside can be had. Much restoration work has taken place in recent times.

Everything at Bolsover is on a large scale as can be

Distant view of Bolsover Castle

seen in the great ruined wings which stretch out along the top of the hill with their enormous doorways and many windows. But as Sacheverell Sitwell has written, Bolsover Castle is '. . . dead as the Mayan ruins of Uxmal or Chichen Itza and as remote from us, but with a ghostly poetry that fires the imagination, that can be never be forgotten and that never cools'.

Although the manor passed out of Cavendish hands through marriage to the Bentincks, Dukes of Portland, their name still proclaims itself locally. There is a huge pub called *The Cavendish Arms* and the parish church of St. Mary has the family punning motto CAVENDO TVTVS carved into an exterior wall. The Cavendish Chapel in the church and its magnificent memorials to Sir Charles and his son the Duke of Newcastle are by Smythson.

The little town itself, though industrial, is not unattractive and has recently undergone some face-lifting. Mining is an important factor in the economy of Bolsover, but at one time it was famous for the manufacture of buckles. The Bolsover buckle was once as famous as a Bakewell pudding or an Aylesbury duck. Tourist information: Chesterfield 823179.

BONSALL *Map G.6*
THIS ATTRACTIVE old village mentioned in Domesday Book and in the midst of former lead mining country is near the celebrated Via Gellia (q.v.). Its church, built upon a hill, is the subject of many tales associated with lead mining. There is an old Market Cross in the town, consisting of a circular shaft on thirteen steps surmounted by a ball. The ceremony of well-dressing is carried on here, several wells being dressed on the last day of the Village Wakes festivities, usually on the Saturday before the first Monday in August. The remains of an extinct volcano are nearby.

BORROWASH *Map L.8*
THE BRICK church, built in 1889-90, is dedicated to St. Stephen and has an eighteenth-century wrought-iron screen attributed to Robert Bakewell of Derby. There are important nurseries in the vicinity. The place is correctly pronounced 'Borrow-ash' and lies within the parish of Ockbrook.

BOYLESTON *Map L.4*
A CHARMING village of quiet by-lanes, 7½ miles south of Ashbourne. Its church has fourteenth-century work and a tower with a pyramidal roof.

BRACKENFIELD *Map G.7*
NINE MILES south of Chesterfield, the agricultural parish of Brackenfield has fine views over the Ogston Reservoir and surrounding countryside. Below the Highoredish ridge on the western boundary of the parish lie the ruins of the medieval Trinity Chapel, whose chancel screen has been preserved in Holy Trinity Church (built in 1856). Within the parish lies Ogston Hall, an 18th century Pickford house with a

The old market cross in the centre of Bonsall

Victorian shell, formerly the seat of the Turbutt family (*vide* Higham), and now of the Wakefields.

BRADBOURNE *Map H.5*

FIVE MILES south-east of Ashbourne, Bradbourne is notable for its church of All Saints, which has Saxon work in the north wall and a Norman tower, while the carving of the south doorway is a rich example of late-Norman sculpture. The font dates from the thirteenth century, the south arcade from about 1300. On the south aisle wall is an unusual seventeenth-century mural painting; the east window is a good early example of nineteenth-century stained glass. In the churchyard is a ninth-century cross shaft carved with a crucifixion. Bradbourne Hall, an Elizabethan house, was once the home of the Buckston family.

BRADLEY *Map J.5*
A VILLAGE of quiet charm in a farmland setting. All Saints' Church has an interesting thirteenth century font and memorials to the Meynells. The Hall is a substantial building at one time the home of a member of the Earl of Cork's family.

BRADWELL *Map D.4*
TWO MILES from Hope, in the famed Hope Valley, nestles the village of Bradwell, with a rocky dale of its own. It includes 'Bagshawe Cavern' (open but see page 24), which contains some very beautiful crystalizations and stalactites. This cavern was discovered in 1800 and is reached by descending 130 steps. New discoveries have been made in recent times. The scenery in the Bradwell district is very impressive and consists of wild crags and overhanging rocks in the highlands of the valley. Two wells are dressed in the village on the first Sunday in August. The church is 19th century.

BRAILSFORD *Map K.5*
A VILLAGE on the Derby-Ashbourne road and the Brailsford brook, a tributary of the Dove, some 6 miles south-east of Ashbourne. At the time of the Domesday Survey, Brailsford is said to have had 'half a church' (due to its position on the boundary of two parishes), and there is a similar entry regarding the adjacent manor of Ednaston (q.v.). The register of All Saints' Church, contains the following entry, which is tragic in its brevity: '1648, Memorandum. CR began his R 1625, March 27th: set up his standard at Nottingham, 22nd August 1642. Beheaded at Whitehall 1649, January 30th.' There are many fine houses in the district including two 20th century country houses – Brailsford Hall and Culland Hall. An annual ploughing match takes place here on the first Wednesday in August.

BRAMPTON *Map E.7* See Old Brampton.

BRASSINGTON *Map H.5*
THE PROXIMITY of quarries does not spoil the fascination of this attractive limestone village full of 17th and 18th century houses set on hilly ground some 800 feet above sea-level and known to the locals as 'Brass'n'. The parish church of St. James has some Norman and even Saxon remains, but Man has left much earlier evidence of his presence hereabouts with prehistoric graves and fragments of a Roman road. Important remains of early mammals found here can be seen in Buxton Museum.

In the church is an unusual memorial to a Yorkshire parson who was passing through sometime in the 18th century during an extremely cold winter. He caught a fever and died and was buried here. Winters are still bad in 'Brass'n'.

The district is full of interest to the geologist and botanist. Rainster Rocks and Harborough Rocks (q.v.) have some curious formations.

BREADSALL *Map K.7*
THE OLD village lies between the Derby-Alfreton and Derby-Heanor roads, not far from Breadsall Priory, a Jacobean house standing on the site of a small settlement of Augustinian Canons, where Dr. Erasmus Darwin (1731-1802), physician, poet and philosopher, lived and died. The Priory has now been converted into a residential hotel incorporating a golf course in the extensive grounds. The club house has facilities for up to 250.

The thirteenth/fifteenth-century church of All Saints has a Norman doorway and the door itself is on carved hinges at least 500 years old. The massive thirteenth-century tower has an elegant fourteenth-century spire. In the north aisle is an exquisitely carved fourteenth-century pietà of alabaster found under the floor of the church in 1877. The church was fired, it is said by suffragettes, in 1914. Some of the old treasures were destroyed, but the building's stone fabric was saved and has been restored.

Nearby is the Old Hall, a building of stone and timber with traces of fourteenth-century work, which was used as a vicarage by John Heiron, a scholarly man who was ejected at the Restoration as a noncomformist. Breadsall Mount, the former Bishops' residence has now been demolished.

BREASTON *Map L.9*
A THRIVING village situated midway between Derby and Nottingham. Housing development in recent years has increased Breaston's popularity as a residential area. The church of St. Michael is a fourteenth-century building with later renovations.

BRETBY *Map N.6*
A VILLAGE with extensive woodlands and charming lanes, mainly residential. Bretby Hall was once one of the most magnificent houses in the county, rivalling Chatsworth. It was built for the 1st Earl of Chesterfield in 1630. The 5th Earl re-built to Wyatville's designs in 1812-13, and now Hall and park are used by the hospital authorities. There is some excellent fishing in the lakes. A magnificent new country seat has been built recently by the Perkins family – Bretby Park. The church of St. Wystan was built in 1877. Close to the village is Brizlincote Hall, built by the 2nd Earl of Chesterfield in 1714. A most unusual building it is now a farmhouse.

BRIMINGTON *Map E.8*
THREE miles north-east of Chesterfield on the road to Worksop, Brimington, like Chesterfield, with which it has had close association over the centuries and now forming part of the Borough of Chesterfield, is described in the Domesday Survey as a *berewick* of the Royal Manor of Newbold. The church of St. Michael was built in 1846.

BROUGH *Map D.4*
REMAINS of the Roman station of *Navio* have been unearthed in a meadow at Brough, near Hope, and many Roman objects found here are now to be seen in Buxton Museum. The fort was probably built in the time of the Emperor Antoninus Pius.

BROWN KNOLL *Map C.2*
A HIGH PEAK moor of 1,866 feet, providing a hardy walkers' approach to Kinder Low (2,077 ft).

Carr of York's famous Crescent at Buxton

BURBAGE *Map E.2*

CHRIST CHURCH, built in 1860 by P. H. Currey, was one of the buildings erected in connection with the seventh Duke of Devonshire's plan for the development as a spa of Buxton, part of which Burbage now is.

BURNASTON *Map M.6*

UNTIL FAIRLY recent times a hamlet of old-world cottages and farms with just a few modern houses, Burnaston is now close to the huge Toyota development. Derby Airport, once here, is now incorporated in the East Midlands International Airport.

BUXTON *Map E.2*

BUXTON IS the Bath of the North. Its warm springs were appreciated by the Romans who called the place Aquae Arnemetiae. Much later Elizabethan courtiers made the hazardous journey to bathe in and drink the waters. From then on many celebrities from Mary Queen of Scots (who came here for 'the cure' while in Lord Shrewsbury's custody) to Noel Coward have come to Buxton on account of its health giving waters.

It was the 5th Duke of Devonshire (husband of the celebrated Georgiana) who really put Buxton on the map. In the 1780s he began a scheme of development which, with later extensions, we can see to this day. The man the Duke commissioned to carry out some of the work was the distinguished architect John Carr – known as 'Carr of York'. He it was who designed the magnificent Crescent, the centrepiece of Buxton. He was also responsible for the other landmark in the town the Devonshire Hospital with its huge dome. This was originally designed as a riding school but became a hospital in 1859 and the dome was added in 1881.

The world of rank and fashion in the north patronised Buxton in the late 18th century but its second great phase occurred in Victorian times. The rise of the middle classes meant that many more could afford the luxury of places like Buxton and many large hotels were built as well as the Pavilion Gardens which were opened in 1871. They contain 23 acres of gardens which include lakes and putting greens in addition to flower beds and shaded walks, whilst children are especially catered for, including the provision of play areas, paddling pools and a miniature railway. The complex of buildings is in the form of a miniature Crystal Palace and includes the Concert Hall, built in iron and glass and opened on 30th August 1876 by the 7th Duke of Devonshire. It is used for meetings, exhibitions, shows and entertain-

Buxton's Victorian Opera House

ments of all kinds and incorporates a restaurant, cafeteria and lounge bar and a conservatory. What was once the old Playhouse theatre is now the Paxton Suite used for seminars etc.

The Opera House, added some years later, has been restored to all its elaborate Victorian splendour as designed by that great theatre architect Frank Matcham. The swimming pool was opened to the public in July 1972 and uses the famous Buxton spa water.

A modern splendour is the Cavendish Arcade designed by Derek Latham. It is not only an architectural gem but also a very popular shopping area.

Sporting facilities in Buxton include two 18-hole golf-courses, Buxton's football team, rugby, hockey, fishing, cycling, rambling, bowling and tennis.

The Slopes in the centre of the town offer relaxation and a vantage point from which to observe the busy town centre. Other attractions are the Serpentine Walks along the banks of the River Wye with its shady walks and seats and Ashwood Park to the east end of Spring Gardens.

The thermal springs rise to the surface at the Natural Baths (now open as the Tourist Information Centre) and are pale blue in appearance when seen in quantity. Perhaps the best place to see and taste the water is at the free well opposite the Crescent. Since recordings were taken the flow from the Springs has been unfailingly consistent both in terms of quantity (32,000 litres per hour) and temperature (27.5° C both winter and summer). The springs rise from almost a mile below the surface and are quite devoid of any unpleasant taste or smell often associated with spa water. Demand for bottled Buxton Water is constantly increasing and it is now available all over the county and beyond.

Buxton today is one of Derbyshire's main holiday resorts and, indeed, one of the main inland resorts in the country, renowned for interesting and invigorating holidays. From its spa era, the town has inherited many hotels and guest-houses, which,

added to its ideal position, make it a natural centre for exploring and enjoying the countryside, including over 500 square miles of National Park which surround it. In recent years the town has also become an important northern conference centre. The Buxton Festival (mainly music) is of international significance and is held in July.

Situated 1,000 feet above sea level, Buxton nevertheless lies in a hollow in the hills at the southern end of the Pennines, near the point where the very nature of those hills changes abruptly. To the north and west are the exhilarating heights of Axe Edge, Bleaklow and Kinder Scout; to the south and east are the world-famous Dales following the courses of the Dove, the Manifold, the Wye and other rivers which cut through the limestone strata.

In addition to The Crescent, part of which has been restored by the Derbyshire County Council for use as an Area Library and offices and the Devonshire Royal Hospital with its remarkable unsupported slate dome, one should not miss the Old Hall Hotel on the site of the Hall which was at times the temporary prison of the unfortunate Mary Queen of Scots; the Tourist Information Centre housed in the former Natural Baths; St. John's Church and many other fine individual or groups of buildings. Nor should one miss the Museum and Art Gallery at the Peak Buildings in Terrace Road where interesting exhibits from Roman times and earlier are to be found, including superb specimens of Blue John (*vide* Castleton) and the Buxton Micrarium, a unique exhibition of Nature under the microscope. It is housed in the old pump room, by the side of St. Ann's Well in the Crescent where the public obtain free supplies of warm mineral water.

In addition to the annual Buxton Festival, the Wells Dressing Festival is held usually in the second week in July, the most important events being the blessing of the wells on the Wednesday and the

Buxton Pavilion Gardens in early Summer

Carnival procession on the Saturday, both of which begin at 2.00 p.m.

Poole's Cavern, Green Lane, Buxton, has been re-opened to the public by the Buxton Civic Association.

The staff at the Tourist Information Centre, The Natural Baths, The Crescent, tel: (0298) 25106, will gladly give every assistance to visitors or prospective visitors; enquiries by letter should be addressed to the Information Officer, Tourist Information Centre, The Crescent, Buxton.

BUXWORTH *Map D.2*
UNTIL THE 1920s this village near Whaley Bridge was called Bugsworth but through a misplaced sense of refinement perhaps mixed with a certain amount of snobbery, the name was changed.
A wag of the time wrote:

Bugsworth bells are ringing
So joyfully and kind,
For Bugsworth now is Buxworth,
Ineffably refined

The old historic name, however, survives in Bugsworth Hall, an early 17th century building. This village was once a centre of lime-burning and the terminus of the old Peak Forest Canal. Relics of Outram's tramway dating from 1800 survive. The church is Victorian with modern stained glass.

CALDWELL *Map O.5*
THIS village of Saxon times takes its name from 'Cold Springs' and was for over four centuries in the possession of Burton Abbey. Caldwell Hall, an eleven-bay brick mansion of distinction, is generally dated *c.* 1712 though a rainwater head bears the date 1678. The Hall and Grange were originally surrounded by a moat cut out of solid rock and the pavement of the Hall courtyard is also of rock. The Hall has been in the possession of many notable families during its existence, the last being the Milligans who descended from the Gresleys. It is now a school for difficult boys.

St. Giles Chapel, though much renewed, still has much Norman work, notably the small round-headed windows on the N side of the nave and chancel and the S side of the nave. It stands in the grounds of the Hall.

CALKE *Map N.7*
DRIVING ALONG the narrow lanes to Calke, one could be back in 1935 if it was not for the pathetic leafless skeletons of dead trees, so typical of our present landscape.

The hamlet is set between the reservoir at Staunton Harold and the great park of Calke Abbey (see pp. 8 & 9). It is a quiet and secret place, an unspoiled and little-known backwater. Long may it so remain.

CALKE ABBEY *Map N.7* see pp. 8 & 9.

CALLOW HALL see under Mapleton

CALLOW *Map J.5*
AGRICULTURAL scattered parish hamlet one mile south west of Wirksworth. Callow Hall is a Victorian farmhouse and not to be confused with the Callow Hall at Mapleton. The name is pronounced 'Caylow'.

CALOW *Map E.8*
A SMALL, residential parish on the eastern outskirts of Chesterfield. The Church of St. Peter (1869) has an unusual steeple and spire.

CALVER *Map E.5*
THE VILLAGE of Calver lies on the west bank of the Derwent, 2 miles north of Baslow and 1 mile from Stoney Middleton. It possesses a fine eighteenth-century bridge which straddles the Derwent but traffic now flows into Calver by way of a new bridge built within sight of the old. It is a favourite rendezvous for walkers and cyclists from Sheffield and Chesterfield and bird lovers can visit the nearby bird gardens. The Derwentwater Arms is reputedly haunted and Calver Mill, built by Arkwright in 1803, is a memorable building. Stoke Hall 1½ miles north west is one of the handsomest of Derbyshire's smaller country houses. It was designed by Richard Booth in 1757 for the Simpson family.

CARSINGTON *Map H.5*
A QUIET village in the hills adjoining Hopton and 2½ miles from Wirksworth possessing an interesting small church rebuilt in 1648 in the Gothic style and dedicated to the Scottish St. Margaret. She is represented in stained glass as is Gellius, the Roman whose funerary urn was found hereabouts, and Philip Lyttelton Gell, who claimed descent from him, dressed as a Saint.

Close to the village is the controversial Carsington Reservoir.

Stained glass window in Carsington Church showing Gellius the Roman and, right, Philip Lyttelton Gell in saintly guise

CASTLE DONINGTON *Map M.8* (See also East Midlands International Airport)

CASTLE DONINGTON, on the Derbyshire/Leicestershire border, is an old village situated on a hill near the River Trent. Many of the houses built on the site of the old castle have good views and many of them have some of the old castle stones in their walls. The church, which dates back to the thirteenth century, contains memorials to the 1st Marquess of Hastings and his wife. He was Governor of India in the early 19th century and his family, the Rawdon-Hastings family, Earls of Moira and Marquesses of Hastings lived in nearby Donington Hall, now the H.Q. of British Midland Airways. Part of the Park containing the old racing track was sold to Mr. T. Wheatcroft who has restored the track and opened a museum containing his own collection of motor racing cars past and present. There are now regular race-meetings in summer.

Castle Donington has become a place of vital importance to the county since the East Midlands International Airport was established.

CASTLE GRESLEY *Map O.6*

LIKE Church Gresley (q.v.) was formerly associated with the Gresley family. It is notable for a large mound known as Castle Knob, the remains of a motte and bailey castle, erected soon after the Conquest by Nigel de Stafford, ancestor of the Gresleys.

CASTLETON *Map C.3*

A CENTRE for Hope Valley, this large village is renowned for its ancient castle and some of Europe's most spectacular caverns which are open to the public. See page 24.

Peveril Castle, ruined and incomplete though it is, has sufficient of its structure remaining to make the steep walk up to it from Castleton well worth while and it is the largest castle of its period to survive in the county. Besides the shell of the keep, much of the curtain wall survives, and within it the foundations of other buildings can be traced. The site, which belongs to the Duchy of Lancaster, is in the care of English Heritage which repairs and maintains the castle in an exemplary fashion.

The castle, perched high above the village, was founded by William Peveril, the Norman adventurer, who saw the inherent strength of its position for the purposes of defence. The present tower, or keep, was erected about 1176, probably to replace an earlier structure, and it was made famous by Sir Walter Scott's *Peveril of the Peak*.

The Church of St. Edmund, practically rebuilt in 1837, has a fine early-Norman chancel arch, good seventeenth-century box pews, and a valuable library including a 'Breeches Bible' of 1611. The library was founded by the Rev. Frederick Farran, who died in 1819, and includes works on divinity, history and biography among other numerous subjects. Later additions have been made by other benefactors. Several monetary bequests made by people during the eighteenth century were devoted to the relieving of distress among the poor.

Before the Norman keep there was a Saxon fortification, for 'ton' is of Anglo-Saxon origin and means 'an enclosure'. An earthwork wall extending in a half moon formation round the village joined the Castle at each end, thus the Castle enclosure became Castleton.

The keep of Peveril Castle

The village is in the centre of the High Peak of Derbyshire, surrounded by hills, dales and valleys bearing names derived from the Celtic denizens of the district.

A custom carried on here commemorates the restoration of Charles II in 1660. The celebration is held on the 29th May, known as Garland Day or Royal Oak Day, when a procession of Morris Dancers led by 'Charles II' and his 'Consort', both in costume and accompanied by a band, threads its way through the town to the Market Place, where the Maypole is plaited and a garland of flowers from the shoulders of the 'King' is hoisted to the top of the church tower.

Other ancient customs which are no longer observed were the Easter morning parade to Castle Hill, to 'see the sun dance', and the hanging of garlands in the village church when the death of a maiden occurred.

Mam Tor, or Shivering Mountain, an escarpment which crumbles in hot weather, the Winnats Gorge, Cave Dale, Hope Valley, and the ancient lead ore mines are notable features. The distinctive part of the village is the remarkable cave formation which has attracted for generations large numbers of visitors.

CATTON HALL *Map O.5*

A LARGE private house by William Smith of Warwick for the Horton family whose descendants still live there. Byron wrote his poem beginning 'She walks in beauty like the night . . .' to one of the ladies of the house.

CHADDESDEN *Map L.7*

See under Derby.

CHAPEL-EN-LE-FRITH *Map D.2*

CHAPEL-EN-LE-FRITH, on the fringe of the old Forest of the Peak, is a small town lying in the north-west angle of Derbyshire on the high land that sweeps up to the High Peak, the highest point of which, Kinder Scout, lies about six miles north.

The town is situated on a high ridge and is surrounded on all sides by lofty hills, the market place standing at an altitude of 776 feet above sea level. It is a picturesque place and attractive by reason of its situation and its old inns, market cross and stocks.

Its name, meaning 'chapel in the forest', is derived from a small chapel, built in 1225 by the keepers of the forest on land bought from the Crown, and dedicated to St. Thomas of Canterbury. The parish church was built in the fourteenth century on the site of the earlier chapel and is a stone building of considerable interest.

Three miles from the town is the Roosdyche, an old track nearly 1,300 paces in length, in the side of the hill, about which many theories are advanced. Ford Hall, in a fine situation, a mile and a quarter north-east, was the ancestral home of the Bagshawes of Derbyshire, the oldest of the Peak families, one of whom was 'The Apostle of the Peak'. Bradshaw Hall has a beautiful Jacobean gateway, bearing the date 1620 and the arms of Francis Bradshaw.

Combs, 2½ miles south-west, was the birthplace, and Chapel-en-le-Frith is now the home of Ferodo brake linings, the chief local industry.

CHARLESWORTH *Map B.1*

RURAL IN character, the cotton mills established in the nineteenth century, having long since ceased to operate. Some two miles away is Melandra Castle, the site of a Roman Fort on the east bank of the River Etherow, which can be reached by a path from the Glossop-Stalybridge road.

CHATSWORTH *Map F.5.* See p. 10.

CHEE DALE *Map E.3*

CHEE DALE, which borders on beautiful Millers Dale, is a magnificent winding gorge, flanked by bare limestone cliffs, which in some places tower 300 feet above the path. Chee Tor is a striking and picturesque landmark, and can only be approached on foot alongside the Wye, from Millers Dale at one end and from Topley Pike at the Buxton end. The high level paths are considered to be dangerous and should be avoided. The upper end is awe-inspiring when seen from the high road climbing Topley and exploration along the riverside reveals a rewarding beauty. See back cover.

CHELLASTON *Map M.7* See under Derby.

CHELMORTON *Map E.3*

THE VILLAGE of Chelmorton may be described as a mountain village, for it is 1,200 feet above sea-level, and is dominated by Chelmorton Low, on which lie two prehistoric barrows. Illy Willy Water, which rises on the Low, passes through the village, disappears in the limestone, and runs undergound for some distance before it again reappears. In the Church of St. John the Baptist there are many interesting relics, the chief of which are stone coffins, the low chancel screen, which dates from the fourteenth century, and the fifteenth-century stone font.

CHESTERFIELD *Map E.7*

CHESTERFIELD, Derbyshire's second town, had its beginnings when the Romans came along the road from Little Chester (Derby) to Templeborough (Yorkshire). By AD 138 it had become the place which may have been known to the Romans as Lutudarum (though Wirksworth also claims this). No doubt it became a trading centre for the adjacent mining areas which, even then, were producing iron and lead. Despite the industrial development that has taken place in Chesterfield, the town is surrounded by some of the most lovely and unspoilt countryside in the county. Moorland areas and open views are found close to the town's boundaries on most approaches.

With the Saxons its importance did not decrease. In the Domesday Book its name is given as Cestrefeld, then a bailiwick of the Royal Manor of Newbold (now a parish on the fringe of the town). Its charter of incorporation as a free borough – with two weekly markets and a fair – was granted by King John in 1204 and regular weekly markets have been held since that time.

In the nineteenth century Chesterfield developed rapidly as an industrial centre and the coming of

Chesterfield's Town Hall. Opposite: Our Lady and All Saints, Chesterfield

George Stephenson set the seal upon its progress. Although he came to Chesterfield comparatively late in life he left his mark upon the town. His principal task at Chesterfield was to supervise the construction of the Midland line through Chesterfield along which today speed the expresses from the north to the west and to London – very different from Robert Stephenson's 30 mph Rocket! He died at Tapton House on 12th August 1848, and was buried in Holy Trinity church.

In the 'Crooked Spire' of the Parish Church of Our Lady and All Saints, Chesterfield possesses one of the architectural curiosities of all time. The spire is 228 feet high, octagonal in plan, and it slopes with an eye-arresting twist. The actual lean when it was last measured was 8 feet $7\frac{3}{4}$ inches to the south, 9 feet $5\frac{3}{8}$ inches to the south-west, and 3 feet $9\frac{1}{2}$ inches to the west. Many reasons have been suggested to explain its crookedness, but it is more than likely that when the church was being constructed, the Black Death was raging and many skilled craftsmen would have died. The survivors, lacking the knowledge of how to season wood satisfactorily, used green timbers for the spire which distorted over the years under the pressure of the heavy lead covering.

The result of this carelessness has, however,

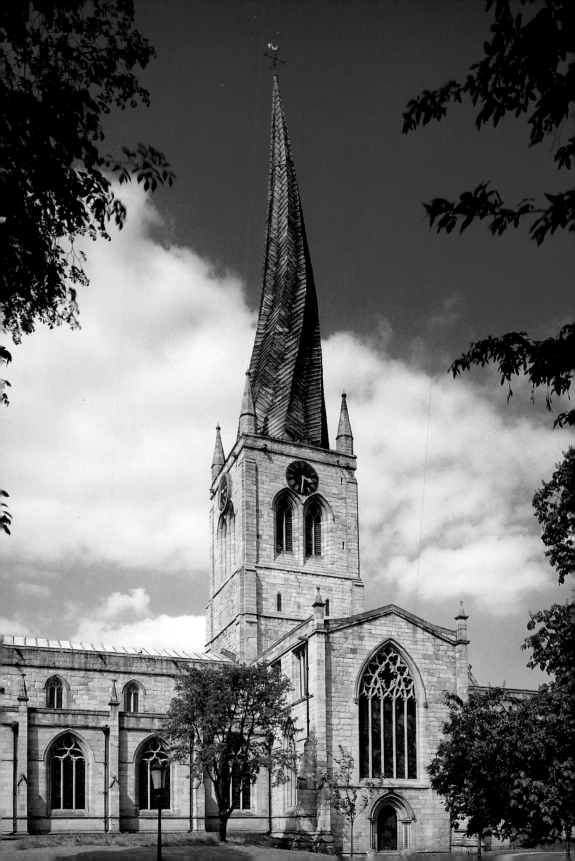

delighted onlookers for centuries!

Its spire apart, the Church of Our Lady and All Saints is one of the most interesting in Derbyshire. It is a fine cruciform building 173 feet long and 100 feet across the transepts. The transepts contain thirteenth-century work, but in the main, the church is fourteenth century in character with some details of a century later.

It has a graceful interior. The font, the oldest feature, dates from Saxon days, and the east end of the church contains four side chapels, one of which, the Lady Chapel, was founded in the thirteenth century by the Guild of St. Mary's – an organisation formed by local residents to protect privileges granted by King John with the manor of Chesterfield to William de Briwere in 1213. Behind the sculptured alabaster altar are the tombs and memorials of the Foljambe family. The lesser Lady Chapel has an unusual architectural feature – a polygonal apse. The other two of the four side chapels originated from the guilds of St. Katherine and of the Holy Cross and in the south wall of the last-named building is a hagioscope – unglazed window – of exceptional size which enabled the members of the guild to see the high altar when seated in their stalls.

The church is unusually rich in old screen work and there are elaborately carved and coloured reredoses at the high altar and in the Holy Cross and St. Peter's Chapels. The church has been enriched by excellent stained glass by Sir Ninian Comper, Christopher Webb and Aldrich Rope.

A disastrous fire, probably the work of an incendiary, occurred just before Christmas Day in 1961, doing damage to the extent of some £40,000. This fire destroyed the fine Schnetzler organ which dated from 1760. The work of restoration included the installation of a new organ, from the former City Hall in Glasgow.

Another interesting link with Chesterfield's past is the Revolution House at Whittington (q.v.).

The disused chapel of the former Royal Manor of Newbold – a suburb of Chesterfield – is also worth a visit although access is difficult. Built as a family chapel for the Eyres, the priest's doorway of this tiny building – it is but 36 feet by 18 feet – is Norman. James II granted its use to the Roman Catholics, but in 1688 it was sacked by a Protestant mob. The chapel closed in 1965 through falling attendances but in 1987 the Chesterfield Civic Society restored it and opened it to the public by prior arrangement with the landlord of the Nag's Head (tel: 232676).

The redevelopment of the town centre, completed in 1981, has provided greatly improved shopping facilities whilst enhancing the character and appearance of the town centre streets and the ancient cobbled Market Place in which is held each Monday,

Friday and Saturday what is reputed to be the largest regular open air market in England and a popular flea-market is also held each Thursday. The Victorian Market Hall, situated in the Market Place, has been magnificently restored to provide up-to-date shopping and a suite of superb assembly rooms which are available for hire and can accommodate a wide variety of functions. Nearby the former Peacock Inn, a medieval timber-framed building, has been sensitively restored and now houses a tourist information centre (telephone 207777/8), a heritage centre where exhibitions of local and national interest are

The Peacock Centre, Chesterfield, for information on the town

displayed and a tourist shop. The Pavements shopping centre contains a unique marriage of new and old; modern premises for a wide variety of shops have been provided without demolishing the old buildings fronting the Market Place. These have been improved with considerable benefit to their surroundings.

Queen's Park is only a few minutes' walk from the bustling Market Place. Bought by public subscription to commemorate Queen Victoria's Golden Jubilee, the Park provides a boating lake with many species of wild fowl, gardens, children's play areas and a cricket ground used regularly by Derbyshire County Cricket Club. A miniature train also runs daily during the Summer.

A modern Sports Centre, opened in 1987 in Queen's Park, provides an impressive array of facilities including squash courts, badminton courts, a fitness room, swimming pools, a waterslide, a health suite and tennis courts. Nearby, in the annexe, is an athletics stadium with running track.

The Stephenson Memorial Hall, opened in 1879, was erected by public subscription in memory of George Stephenson. The building now houses the Civic Theatre. The public library is now housed in a modern building attached to the Pavements Shopping Centre. It incorporates the Children's Library and School libraries.

Chesterfield is close to the M1 and can boast excellent communications from all directions by both road and rail. The Midland Railway Station is within a short distance of the town centre, a comprehensive bus service is provided by private operators and by-passes have been built on the major roads to the north and south-east of the town. These, together with the town centre by-pass will help to ensure a trouble-free journey for the private motorist. There is plenty of inexpensive car parking space available within easy reach of all points of interest in the town.

Chesterfield is ideally situated for use as a centre for visiting the magnificent countryside of the Peak District and the superb historic houses at Chatsworth, Haddon and Hardwick.

Chesterfield's concert and conference centre, the Winding Wheel, which has been renovated to the highest possible standards, provides an ideal venue for tea dances, lectures, concerts and exhibitions. The Centre is administered by the Borough Council, can seat up to 900 and is available for public hire. As well as the Main Hall, there is a Ballroom and separate Function Room.

The town has excellent opportunities for sport and has a reputation as a sports centre. The Chesterfield Football Club plays in the League Fourth Division and there are numerous amateur teams in the neighbourhood. The Derbyshire County Cricket Club plays many of its matches each season at Queen's Park and there are a number of other clubs in the district, some of which participate in league cricket.

Golf courses in the vicinity are located at Tapton (Chesterfield Municipal) and at Walton (Chesterfield Golf Club) – both 18 holes and there is a nine-hole course at Stanedge. Tennis, bowls, badminton, swimming and boating are all catered for.

The Pomegranate Theatre has been refurbished and provides a wide variety of different types of entertainment. See page 7.

CHINLEY *Map C.2*

FORMERLY an important railway junction on the main London-Manchester line, with a branch line through Hope Valley to Sheffield, Chinley is a convenient centre for exploring the north Derbyshire hills, including Eccles Pike and Chinley Churn. The two huge railway viaducts have been described by the Rev. Henry Thorold as 'one of the greatest monuments to Victorian Industrial England'.

CHISWORTH *Map B.1*

A SMALL hamlet situated one mile south-west of Charlesworth. Nearby are the Cown Edge Rocks and two stone monoliths known as 'Robin Hood's Picking Rods' and 'The Abbot's Chair'.

CHURCH BROUGHTON *Map L.4*

A QUIET agricultural village, 10 miles west of Derby and a centre of fine pastoral scenery. St. Michael's Church, though mainly of the fourteenth century, also possesses Norman work.

CHURCH GRESLEY *Map O.6*

THE GREAT family who held their lands continuously in the male line from the 11th to the 20th century and from which this village derived its name has ceased to exist. Their castle is but a grass-covered hummock (*vide* Castle Gresley) and their later seat, Drakelow, has long since been demolished.

In the church, which incorporates fragments of the Augustinian priory, is a fine monument to Sir Thomas Gresley showing heraldically the many alliances of his family. Alas, that family is now 'entombed in the urns and sepulchres of mortality'.

CHURCH WILNE *Map M.8*

See under Draycott

CLAY CROSS *Map G.8*

CLAY CROSS has had a very bad press in recent years and it might come as a surprise to someone visiting the town for the first time to see that it is not at all an unpleasant place, that the hammer and sickle does not fly from every window and that the air is fresh and bracing.

An unabashed industrial centre with no pretentions to beauty or the picturesque, Clay Cross is well placed on the A61 south of Chesterfield, occupying a commanding position on a high ridge between the valleys of the rivers Amber and Rother. Mining was the industry here but ironworks and engineering are replacing it as the main source of employment.

George Stephenson was the man who developed Clay Cross in the last century. He discovered coal while building the Clay Cross Tunnel (the castellated entrance to which is an interesting relic of railway architecture) and founded the Clay Cross Company. He even instituted a primitive form of welfare state to improve the lot of his workpeople. It worked well. The Company was later to call in Alfred Stevens to design the present large and distinguished parish church in 1851.

CLIFTON *Map K.4*

A CHARMING village, with a nine-hole golf course, 1¼ miles south-west of Ashbourne. Hanging Bridge, a picturesque structure over the Dove, on the main Ashbourne-Leek road, is within the parish.

Clifton's principal attraction is the fine unhedged road crossing the deer park of Okeover on the Staffordshire bank of the Dove. Wooded slopes lead steeply to the hilly range which also forms the western bank of the Manifold Valley. This is perhaps the most pleasant approach to both Dovedale and the Manifold Valley for motorists and ramblers alike. For the latter there is reserved an enchanting stroll along the side of the Dove from Okeover to the very entrance of the dale.

CLOWNE *Map E.9*

THIS COLLIERY village sprawls along the Nottinghamshire border. Fine countryside walks abound in the district and there is angling to be had at the Harlesthorpe Dam. There is a market cross in the village. The church of St. John the Baptist, located somewhat unusually away from the traditional village centre, was built originally in Norman style but partially rebuilt in the Early English and Perpendicular periods. The register dates from 1569 but is in bad condition.

COAL ASTON *Map D.7*

THIS FORMER mining village is now almost joined up with Dronfield (q.v.). It has quaint narrow alleys and a village cross. There is no Anglican church but there are two dissenting chapels. The Chequers Inn, an 18th century hostelry, is now a steak house.

CODNOR *Map J.8*

HERE ARE the ruins of a once great castle built by the Greys in the reign of Henry III upon the site of an earlier fortress erected by Robert de Morteyne. There was a great park of 2,000 acres and the building had two large courtyards, four massive towers, a noble gateway and a deep moat. The ruins today include a boundary wall of one of the courtyards, portions of the towers, a quaint stone dovecote and other remnants. Several of the local farms and cottages incorporate in their structure some of the castle's ancient stone, and of these Breach Farm is particularly interesting. A site of war-time prefabricated dwellings has been cleared and a group bungalow scheme with warden supervision has been erected on part of the land. The remainder has been developed privately both individually and in bulk.

COMBS *Map D.2*

A SMALL rural village nestling in the valley. Nearby is Combs Reservoir which looks more like a natural lake and provides scenic views for the walker, excellent sailing and fishing.

COTMANHAY *Map K.9*

THIS IS now part of Ilkeston but has its own small church of the 1840s with a bell-turret.

COTON-IN-THE-ELMS *Map O.5*

ONE OF the smaller parishes in the South Derbyshire area and largely agricultural in character, though the now defunct collieries were not far away. The parish church was built in 1846.

COXBENCH *Map J.7*

THIS TINY hamlet even had a railway station in the Golden Age of Steam. The small building still exists but the main object of attention is Coxbench Hall, a modest 18th century building with poorly proportioned window space (a rare fault at that period) and fine stables. It was once the home of William Brooks Johnson, MD whose memorial can be found in the church at near-by Horsley (q.v.) The writer and journalist Rosemary Meynell was born here.

CRESSBROOK *Map E.4*

A LEAFY, wooded place with glorious views, a curious Gothick chapel and a fine old mill (1815) once owned by the carpenter-poet William Newton. Anna Seward christened him 'The Minstrel of the Peak'. Cressbrook Dale is also very beautiful and contains Peter's Stone, a freakish outcrop of limestone.

CRESWELL CRAGS *Map E.10*

A BEAUTIFUL ravine close to the Nottinghamshire borders and the Dukeries with Permian limestone cliffs where the river has the appearance of a long lake. Remains of Palaeolithic Man of the greatest scientific importance have been discovered in caves in the cliffs, along with bones of the mammoth and several artistically carved bones of great interest. Some are preserved in the British Museum, Derby Museum and Sheffield Museum. Near-by Creswell was developed with the sinking of Creswell Colliery in the 1890s. For the Heritage Centre see page 7.

CRICH *Map H.7*

A VILLAGE of much character so set upon the hills as to offer magnificent views in almost every direction. Crich Stand, the war memorial of the Sherwood Foresters (Nottinghamshire and Derbyshire

Approaching Cressbrook Dale

Regiment), a tower with beacon light, 950 feet above sea level, was opened in 1923 on the site of two previous towers. The annual pilgrimage of the regiment to the memorial, with a service at 3 p.m., is held on the first Sunday in July.

Crich Tramway Museum houses numerous interesting trams many of which are in working order and give rides to visitors at weekends and Bank Holidays from April to October. Here will be seen the façade of Robert Adam's beautiful Derby Assembly Rooms, damaged by fire and subsequently demolished – a grievous loss to the City's architecture. See page 5.

St. Mary's Church, consecrated in 1135, has Norman arcades to the nave and a massive circular Norman font. The chancel, with excellent windows and triple sedilia, the aisles, and the tower and spire were all rebuilt in the fourteenth century, when also the nave was lengthened. The tower parapet has a curious band of wavy lines similar to those at Chesterfield and Denby. On the north chancel wall is a stone Bible rest, of which there are several in Derbyshire, though few elsewhere. In the north aisle is the recessed tomb of Sir William de Wakebridge, who founded a chantry here and whose family was wiped out in the Black Death.

CROMFORD *Map H.6*

THIS VILLAGE built among fine rock scenery in the Derwent Valley is distinguished for its association with the early years of the Industrial Revolution and in particular with Sir Richard Arkwright, who established here his first water-powered cotton mill fed by local streams in 1771, and built the village (the first of a notable line of factory villages) to house his workpeople. Now over 200 years old, the Mill is a justly famous one. It was the first factory in the world where a major source of power (water) was utilised. It thus became the birthplace of the technique of mass production – the key to the Industrial Revolution – which has since changed the face and the living standards of the world. Willersley Castle, a very fine 18th century house and former home of the Arkwrights, is now a Methodist Guest House.

A fine fifteenth-century bridge across the Derwent has pointed arches on one side and rounded on the other. A tiny fishing temple with the dedication

Cromford and its pool

Sir Richard Arkwright

'Piscatoribus Sacrum' stands close to the bridge. At the south end are some remains of an unusual bridge chapel. The Church of St. Mary, close by, rebuilt in 1859, contains memorials of the Arkwrights. Cromford is an excellent fly-fishing centre, and good for rock climbing.

The unique High Peak Railway, built over 140 years ago, terminated near Cromford with a gradient of 1 in $8\frac{1}{2}$ on the Sheep-Pasture section. Originally intended to connect the Peak Forest Canal at Whaley Bridge with the Cromford Canal, the line has now been opened to the public as a Trail for walkers and horse riders.

The station, which is still in use, is a little master-piece of railway architecture attributed to G. H. Stokes, the son-in-law of Sir Joseph Paxton.

Cromford Steam Fair is an annual event held in Cromford Meadows. This is also the venue for other events throughout the year. One of Arkwright's mills is now a museum and the Cromford Canal Society runs regular boat trips from the wharf. These are horse-drawn barges and one of the stops is at Lea Wood Pump House, now restored and in working order. Cromford also has a trout farm. See also *Black Rocks* and page 5.

CROWDECOTE *Map F.3*

THIS ATTRACTIVE hamlet, on the Derbyshire bank of the upper Dove, is near wild and bracing hill country. It was mentioned in the Domesday Book as Cruda's Cot and relics of Saxon days when Cruda owned the land can be found in the locality of the Pack Horse Inn.

CUBLEY *Map L.4*

ST. ANDREW'S Church, dating from the twelfth-thirteenth centuries, possesses many ancient monuments. From this village came Michael Johnson who became a book-seller in Lichfield. He was the father of Dr. Samuel Johnson.

CURBAR *Map E.5*

'HAS ANY village in Derbyshire a finer outlook' asks Arthur Mee with much justification, as the views are memorable. The church was built to the designs of the younger Salvin; there is a curious old lock-up and by the river is Calver Mill (*vide* Calver).

CUTTHORPE *Map E.7*

THIS PLEASANT village forms part of the parish of Old Brampton and lies on the B6030. It has two historic halls, the Old Manor House, a three storied building with attached stair tower, which was once the property of the Sitwell family and was built by Ralph Clarke, the first Mayor of Chesterfield in 1625 and Cutthorpe Hall *c.* 1675 which was once the house of the Heathcote family. The Linacre reservoirs also lie partly within the village boundaries.

DALBURY *Map L.5*

DALBURY and its companion, Dalbury Lees, are two scattered villages in a farming community. The church is a remote place and was restored by Charles Evelyn Cotton. In the nave is a lancet window with a piece of 13th century stained glass depicting a figure of St. Michael. The dedication is to All Saints and the church possesses some good plate.

DALE ABBEY *Map L.8*

THE WHOLE area known as Dale Abbey has been described as a 'Derbyshire Shangri-La' and rightly so. It is a haven surrounded by the urban sprawl and industry of Long Eaton, Staveley, Ilkeston and Sandiacre yet within its green folds one could be a thousand miles away from industrialisation. Its survival is something of a miracle.

The district is named after the now ruined Abbey of St. Mary formerly a large Premonstratensian monastery. The main fragment is the chancel east

The Chancel arch of Dale Abbey

The post Windmill at Dale Abbey

window but the outline can be seen of some of the buildings and one or two pieces of masonry survive in local houses as the ruins were used as a quarry for years. There is a mysterious hermit's cave and a working post windmill but the gem of Dale Abbey is the tiny Church of All Saints. The building is part church and part farmhouse (the farmhouse was once a pub). The church contains a medieval wall painting and a jumble of box pews. The pulpit, reading desk and clerk's pew are all behind the altar and this is the only instance where this arrangement is found in a church still in use.

DARLEY ABBEY *Map L.7.* See under Derby.

DARLEY DALE *Map G.6*
ENCOMPASSING North Darley and South Darley, Darley Dale connects Rowsley and Matlock, and the hill and valley scenery is broad and open though a century of ribbon development has left its scars. Fly-fishing in this neighbourhood is popular, and several large clubs fish the Derwent, including the Sheffield Waltonian Club. The Church of St. Helen dates from the twelfth century and contains a Burne-Jones window and a peal of eight bells, dating from 1618. The famous old yew tree, one of the thickest in England, has a girth of 33 feet at four feet from the ground.

The well-known Stancliffe stone quarries and the famous Mill Close lead mines (now no longer worked owing to flooding) are situated in Darley. Sir Joseph Whitworth (1803-87), the engineer and inventor, lived the last fifteen years of his life at Stancliffe Hall (now a preparatory school for boys). The Whitworth Hospital, founded by his widow, is at Darley Dale. The dale is an excellent centre from which to tour a very lovely part of Derbyshire.

The 19th century Darley Dale Hydro is now St. Elphin's School for Girls.

DENBY *Map J.8*
HERE was the birthplace, in 1646, of John Flamsteed, the first Astronomer Royal. Now renowned for its modern decorated glazed earthenware. The Church of St. Mary, thirteenth-century, has a broach spire and interesting pierced pointed trefoils. The arcade is the oldest surviving part of the church and has two bays. See also *Shipley*.

DERBY *Map L.7*
THE FACE of Derby, the county town, has changed considerably during the last hundred years. Already a major industrial and commercial centre, the town at last received city status as formal recognition of its size and worth, when Letters Patent were presented by Her Majesty Queen Elizabeth II, on 28th July, 1977. Derby has expanded rapidly, spreading out over the surrounding hills and embracing many of the villages which once stood on its fringe. It has a fine market hall and attractive gardens along the river bank. The monument to Sir Henry Royce, a pioneer of the motor industry, which once stood here is now at the Rolls Royce H.Q. at Sinfin. There are over one hundred parks, playing fields and open spaces in the city, the oldest of which is the Arboretum given to the city by Joseph Strutt in 1840. Sadly in recent years many of Derby's fine buildings have been destroyed, though some fine new ones have redressed the balance.

Little more than 80 years ago, the great works of the Midland Railway provided Derby's only significant claim to industrial importance. But so rapid has been progress that the city is now one of the most prosperous in Britain.

Derby has a history dating back to the Roman occupation with a fort on the west side and a town on the east side of the River Derwent. On the eastern bank stood Derventio, in the area now known as Little Chester. Sometime between AD 655 and AD 800 a minster church was founded as the evangelizing centre for a vast royal estate called Northworth(y). In AD 800 or thereabouts, St. Alkmund was brought from his native Northumbria for burial here to avoid the Vikings. A major settlement surrounded the church. In AD 874, the Vikings occupied the area, reinforced the Roman walls of Derventio and changed the name to 'Deoraby' or 'Der-aby'.

In 917, King Aethelflaeda of Mercia expelled the Danes, and some ten years later a new Minster church (All Saints') was founded and the burgh of Derby was founded with its own mint.

Between AD 924 and 931 Derby was once again occupied by the persistant Danes.

By the time that Domesday Book was compiled, Derby had become a town of at least 2,000 inhabitants. Fourteen mills are mentioned and six churches, two of them collegiate, but at least two others existed at that time: St. Helen's and St. James's. Yet from this time until about 1760 there can have been little material expansion.

In 1954 Derby celebrated the 800th anniversary of the granting of a charter by Henry II giving the people the right to hold markets. Other charters followed, the last one in 1682, by Charles II.

Less than a century later Derby was in the throes of a rebellion around which have been woven more

Derby Museum and Art Gallery in the Wardwick. Opposite: Derby Cathedral

romantic stories than it probably deserved. Bonnie Prince Charlie's army, pipes playing and standards flying, entered the town in 1745, despite the fact that the Duke of Devonshire had raised a force to meet it. The Prince himself arrived in the evening, despondent that the substantial moneys and men he had expected to receive from the sympathetic Colonel Pole, of Radburne Hall, and other Derbyshire adherents were not forthcoming; the Prince's generals, against his wishes, decided that discretion was the better part of valour and a retreat was ordered (*Vide* Swarkstone).

The year 1817 saw three rebels hanged at the county gaol – the leaders of a revolt at Pentrich, a Derbyshire hill village. Sixteen years later the town saw another revolt: its scene was Messrs. Peet and Frost in Bridge Street (now the Rykneld Mills). There had been trouble at the mill for some time with 'Luddite' raids, unemployment and sweated labour: but it was on 23rd November, 1833, that the management's decision to refuse employment to trade union members caused a complete revolt. The strike lasted until March the following year. At this period there was much unrest throughout the country, for two years previously serious rioting had broken out in many towns, including Derby, when the House of Lords rejected the Reform Bill of 1831. Near-by Markeaton Hall was stormed by a rabble and windows were broken.

The fine wrought-iron gates by Robert Bakewell to the old Silk Mill have been moved back beside it, close to their original site. Other interesting buildings (some with modern shop fronts) will be found in the Market Place, Iron Gate, Wardwick, Sadler Gate and St. Mary's Gate, in Queen Street (notably, the sixteenth-century timber-framed Dolphin Inn) and especially in Friar Gate, which is considered as one of the finest surviving Georgian townscapes in the Midlands.

Not far away is the magnificent tower of the Cathedral, rising above the centre of the city. Surmounted by four pinnacles at the angles, the 178-foot tower was built between 1511 and 1531. After Boston Stump it is the highest tower in England built for a parish church. It is a magnificently rich specimen of late perpendicular with a great clock by John Whitehurst who rebuilt the original one by George Ashmore in 1745. The clock was electrified by John Smith and Sons, diagonally opposite. A carillon chimes at regular intervals. All Saints became the Cathedral in 1927.

The tower apart, the Cathedral was rebuilt by James Gibbs (the designer of St. Martin-in-the-Fields and of the Radcliffe Library at Oxford) largely through the efforts of an eighteenth-century vicar, Dr. M. Hutchinson, who had the old church pulled down almost overnight. The new building was completed two years later and, as an inscription in the

The Guildhall, Derby

Opposite: James Gibbs's classical interior of Derby Cathedral

Consistory Court states, Dr. Hutchinson preached the first sermon on 21st November, 1725.

After the tower, the Cathedral's chief features are the superb wrought-iron screen fashioned by the celebrated Robert Bakewell, and the lovely little Cavendish chapel. Here, in addition to many of the Earls and Dukes of Devonshire, lies the Countess of Shrewsbury the autocratic and much-married 'Bess of Hardwick' – builder of many mansions. A great and magnificently carved tomb, made entirely from Derbyshire marbles and designed by Robert Smythson is her memorial.

Here, too, lie Henry Cavendish, the brilliant chemist and philosopher, John Lombe, the silk mill builder, and Lt. Gen. Cavendish who died on the battlefield at Gainsborough in 1643. In the south aisle is a rare wooden tomb of a canon of about 1500, with a row of weepers on the side and the remains of a cadaver below. There are other monuments by Roubiliac, Rysbrack, Nollekens, Chantrey and Westmacott. The Roubiliac is to the Chambers family, a Mrs. Chambers having given Derby its first street lighting in 1738. It has Bakewell ironwork. The interesting Bishop's throne, of the seventeenth-eighteenth centuries, came from Asia Minor and was presented to the cathedral by a Derbyshire clergyman. The wrought-iron gates at the entrance to the cathedral, dedicated in 1958, are the work of Robert Bakewell. They formerly stood in front of a house in St. Mary's Gate that belonged to the Osborne family

(whose arms surmount them). This building, converted into a Baptist chapel in 1841, was demolished in 1938 and the gates were subsequently purchased with the co-operation of the Friends of the Cathedral and carefully restored.

To the north of the Cathedral is the church of St. Michael, rebuilt in 1858 and after being in danger of demolition was rescued in the 1980s and skillfully converted to an architect's studio and offices. To the north is the Roman Catholic Church of St. Mary, built by Pugin in 1838, with a tower 117 feet high. St. Mary's Church looks down on St. Alkmund's Way, a section of the Inner Ring Road, constructed on the site of St. Alkmund's Church, during the demolition of which a magnificent carved stone sarcophagus, possibly that of St. Alkmund, was excavated, and is now on display in Derby Museum. The landscaping of St. Alkmund's Way won a Civic Trust Award in 1969.

St. Mary's Gate, passing the seventeenth-century Shire Hall, leads towards Cheapside and St. Werburgh's (founded in AD 699), which has a register dating back to 1583 and containing the entry of Dr. Samuel Johnson's marriage to Tetty Porter, when the couple raced to the church from Birmingham on 9th July, 1735. There is a pelican lectern of 1711 and a bishop's chair representing the church's patron saint made by a craftsman at Tideswell. The church was rebuilt in 1893 by Sir Arthur Blomfield, except for the tower of 1601 and

Friargate with Joseph Pickford's house on the right

the chapel of 1699 (formerly the chancel), which contains a memorial by Chantrey to Sarah Whinyates (d. 1828). The Blomfield nave has been attractively converted to a shopping mall and is now known as St. Werburgh's Cloisters.

St. Peter's Church has some Norman masonry (the oldest in the city) and has recently been the subject of considerable restoration.

In the quiet churchyard was the first Derby School, until lately used as the Church Institute. A Tudor house originally, it housed the school for more than 300 years and its pupils included John Cotton, one of the Pilgrim Fathers, John Flamsteed, the first Astronomer Royal, and 'Wright of Derby', the eighteenth-century painter who refused academic honours but of whose powers there is ample evidence in the pictures which hang in the city's Art Gallery comprising the largest collection of Wrights.

The ancient chapel standing on St. Mary's Bridge – once called 'St. Mary on the Brigge' and a haven for travellers entering and leaving the city when the bridge was the only means of crossing the Derwent – was restored in 1930 by the Derbyshire Archaeological Society and has now been dedicated to perpetual sacred use in association with the Cathedral. One of the six remaining medieval bridge chapels in England, it dates mainly from the fifteenth century.

Several schemes for development of the city centre have now been completed, including sections of the Inner Ring Road, pedestrianisation schemes and the building of the Eagle Centre which contains a shopping precinct, market, public house, car park and

a theatre building housing the Derby Playhouse company. The theatre, situated imposingly at the head of the Eagle Centre market, is financed by the Arts Council, Derby City Council and the East Midlands Arts Association. It was designed by Roderick Ham, and the auditorium seats approximately 550, including provision for the disabled and sound amplification facilities for the deaf. The building also includes a restaurant.

The new Assembly Rooms in the Market Place cater for a wide range of functions including banquets, concerts, dances and exhibitions.

The importance of education has always been recognised in the county and excellent facilities exist in and about the city for children and students of all ages. Since the war a comprehensive scheme of new building and re-organisation has been carried out, and many new primary and secondary schools, together with four new special schools have been opened.

The demand for improved standards of education is now served by the Derbyshire College of Higher Education (formed by an amalgamation of the Bishop Lonsdale College of Education and the Kedleston Road College of Art and Technology) and the College of Further Education situated at Wilmorton. The Youth Service, work for the Duke of Edinburgh's Award and Adult Evening Centres are also actively promoted. Tertiary Colleges are at Wilmorton and Mackworth.

Multi-screen cinemas are at Osmaston Park Road and at the Meteor Centre. The city has its own

Concert Orchestra, Bach Choir, a Choral Union and many other clubs and societies. Concerts are held frequently and these usually feature well-known artists. In June 1971, the Queen Mother officially opened the Guildhall as a concert theatre and club centre and in November 1977 she again visited Derby to open the new Assembly Rooms. Built by Casson, Conder and Partners, the new Assembly Rooms have a Great Hall to accommodate up to 1,850 people for concerts and receptions and the Darwin Suite for more intimate functions. The Assembly Rooms are the most dramatic contribution to Derby's architecture this century but much of the new building of the late 1980s and early 1990s reverts back to more attractive traditional designs.

Self portrait of Joseph Wright, Derbyshire's most distinguished painter

1979 was the centenary year of the Museum and Art Gallery building, which has been greatly extended over the years. The Art Gallery has the finest collection of paintings by Joseph Wright of Derby, and an unrivalled collection of Derby Porcelain. The Museum holds collections of Derbyshire antiquities, natural and social history and the largest collection of clocks by John Whitehurst F.R.S. (1713-1788) and his family. It is also the official museum of the 95th (Derbyshire) Regiment, the Derbyshire Yeomanry and the 9th/12th Lancers. A working layout illustrating the history of the Midland Railway is now in the Museum of Industry, housed in the old Silk Mill on the banks of the Derwent. The Museum of Industry also displays a Rolls-Royce aero engine collection and other displays showing the development of local industrial history. The Royal Crown Derby Porcelain Co Ltd, has a museum at its factory with displays of the products of the Company (see page 6).

For details of Pickford's House Museum in Friar Gate, see page 5.

Sport too is admirably catered for. Derby County Football Club needs no introduction. In addition, rugby football, hockey, tennis, bowls, rowing, fishing and hunting – the famous Meynell and South Staffs Hunt often meets within five miles of the city – are all served. There are four golf courses at hand – two of them municipally owned. The indoor Sports Centre at Moor Lane provides excellent facilities for most indoor sporting activities. An adjacent building houses a first-class swimming pool.

There is a Tourist Information Centre. Tel: 2931111 and ask for the appropriate extension.

Although the Hall has been demolished, Markeaton Park is one of the finest of Derby's many open spaces for boating, fishing and children's recreation.

In the 1920s and 1930s Derby was twinned with Foucquvilliers in France but since the early 1970s its twin city is Osnabrück in Germany – hence Osnabrück Square.

Derby covers an area of thirty square miles, city districts include:

Artist's impression of the Toyota factory

DERBY SUBURBS

Allestree *Map L.7*
THE CHURCH of St. Edmund, largely Victorian, has a low thirteenth-century tower and part of the east wall of the chancel was erected at about the same time. The principal glory is the Norman doorway inside the timber porch. Under the fourteenth-century arch is a stone engraved with a cross which may have covered the grave of a Christian who lived long before the church was built. Part of a piscina is 700 years old. There are several memorials of the 17th and 18th centuries to the Mundys of Markeaton, and to the Evans and the Johnsons of Allestree Hall.

Allestree Park was once the estate of the Evans family and is now one of the loveliest public parks, with a fine 18-hole golf course and a collection of birds.

Alvaston and Boulton *Map M.7,8*
THE PARISH CHURCH of St. Michael was rebuilt on the site of an ancient chapelry. Under the old tower was found a pre-Norman sepulchral slab, now in the church. A striking piece of beaten ironwork, depicting St. Michael, is attributed to Robert Bakewell, the eighteenth-century Derby ironsmith. There is a fourteenth-century piscina. The font was a thanks-offering for the capture of Sebastopol.

Darley Abbey *Map L.7*
OF THE formerly separate villages which surrounded Derby, Darley Abbey is the closest to the city centre and has grown into a flourishing suburb.

The only substantial fragment of the Abbey to survive has been carefully and tastefully restored and is now a popular public house.

Darley Park, landscaped by William Emes, has attractive flower beds, shrubberies and lawns running down to a stretch of the Derwent which is used for boating and for an annual regatta. The hall, built in 1727 but now demolished, was for 120 years the home of the Evans family who built the cotton mill on the river in 1783.

Chaddesden *Map L.7*
THE CHURCH contains a rood screen and an unusual chalice-shaped font 600 years old. The fine linenfold panelling of the sanctuary and the oak and alabaster reredos are in memory of Sir Henry Wilmot, who won the VC at Lucknow. The Wilmots lived for many years at Chaddesden Hall, which has now disappeared, though part of the Park remains.

Chellaston *Map M.7*
THIS IS now a residential area with many new houses but once the alabaster from its quarries was in great demand and many monumental effigies in the Midlands are made from Chellaston alabaster.

Littleover *Map M.6, 7*
LITTLEOVER lies off the Derby-Burton and Derby-Uttoxeter roads, a few minutes journey from Derby city centre.

The church of St. Peter has a Norman doorway and font, with fourteenth century windows in the chancel and south aisle. An outstanding seventeenth century memorial depicts Sir Richard Harpur and his wife kneeling together at a desk. The Old Hall was built by his father and demolished in 1891. Its replacement, built in 1891 is the headquarters of the County Fire Brigade. There is an old cottage in Littleover Hollow which is said to have contained some remnants of a Norman dwelling. Derby High School for Girls is situated here.

Within this parish is the Pastures, a fine Regency mansion by the architect Richard Leafer set in a spacious park with a lake. The house is now used as a hospital.

Mackworth *Map L.6*
A COLLECTION of pretty 17th and 18th century houses grouped around a small green at the west gates of Markeaton Park (112 acres landscaped by William Emes), former seat of the Mundy family. Although the Hall has gone, there is a fine orangery by Pickford which survives.

All Saints Church, Mackworth

The fourteenth-century church contains a fine alabaster slab commemorating Thomas Touchet, rector from 1381 to 1409 and an elaborately carved lectern of 1903 – a fantasy of vine-leaves and grapes.

Along the village street, which is connected to the main Derby-Ashbourne road by a pleasant sunken lane, is a Gothic gatehouse, called Mackworth Castle.

Mickleover *Map L, M.6*
THIS RAPIDLY expanding suburb has a fine fourteenth century church, dedicated to All Saints, some attractive cottages and pastoral views of undulating country to the wooded surroundings of Radburne Hall.

The timber-framed Old Hall was built for a Cromwellian Officer in 1648 and the Victorian manor house by the church was designed by Henry Duesbury in 1849.

Spondon *Map L.8*
A SUBURB situated four miles east of the centre of Derby which has grown rapidly since the estab-lishment there of the extensive works of the British Celanese Company (now part of Courtaulds, the textile and rayon manufacturers). St. Werburgh's Church, with registers from 1580, has a portion of an Anglo-Saxon cross in the churchyard.

In Sitwell Street stands The Homestead, a magni-ficent brick house built in 1741 in Queen Anne style. It is one of Derby's six Grade I listed buildings.

Lea Rhododendron Gardens

DERWENT DALE *Map B.4* See under Ladybower.

DETHICK, LEA AND HOLLOWAY
Map H.6
A COMBINED parish of three hamlets, 2½ miles from

Cromford, includes Lea Hurst, for many years the home of Florence Nightingale and now a home for old people. Lea Rhododendron Gardens are open to the public (tel: 0629 534380). There are spinning and hosiery mills at Lea. At Dethick lived Anthony Babington, who was executed for his share in the Babington Plot for the release of Mary Queen of Scots

Florence Nightingale

Opposite: Entrance to Dovedale.

Below: a wood near Holloway under winter snow

from captivity. St. John the Baptist Church dates partly from the thirteenth century. Displayed around the tower of 1539 there are heraldic shields carved in stone, which recall the various marriage alliances of the Babingtons. A near-by farmhouse incorporates parts of the old hall in which the family lived.

DEVIL'S ELBOW *Map A.2*
TRAVELLING through Longdendale Valley the Devil's Elbow lies on the right, the Derbyshire side, and to the left, on the Cheshire side, is Crowden Moor, giving access to the Brushes and Mossley. The television mast of Holme Moss is in the area.

There are splendid views of the series of reservoirs along the valley, and the rugged slopes of the hills beyond.

DINTING *Map A.1*
THE RAILWAY used to dominate this community on the outskirts of Glossop. The huge viaduct carrying

the Sheffield-Manchester line was built in 1845 and there was once a railway museum here. The church of Holy Trinity was built in 1875 by a firm of architects sounding like a North Country music hall turn – Mills and·Murgatroyd.

DOVEDALE *Map H.3*
THE VALLEY of the Dove, together with that of its neighbour, the Manifold, forms part of the Peak District National Park. Considerable portions of the area have come either by private gift, public subscription or covenants into the hands of the National Trust. The generosity of Sir Robert and Lady McDougall, Mr. E. H. Kerfoot, Mr. F. A. Holmes, and of Imperial Chemical Industries, are especially to be remembered.

In Dovedale the river Dove runs through a narrow limestone gorge where steep tree-covered walls rise high above the stream. In places the action of water has worn away the rock into curious formations like the Lion's Head and the natural archway in front of Reynard's Cave. There are fine views from the heights, such as Thorpe Cloud and Bunster, which overlook the valley.

A dozen fascinating and beautiful villages are included in the area. All can be reached by car, but to discover the best of the dales or the hilltops one must of necessity walk. The villages have their old halls, Tudor houses and interesting customs. Traces of Roman encampments and roads are to be found, together with the stone monuments and the burial mounds and chambers of early man.

The gorge of Dovedale proper stretches for only two miles above Thorpe. However, the next six miles upstream, through Milldale, Wolfscote Dale and Beresford Dale to Hartington, will also amply reward with their beauty the efforts of the walker. So, too, will the eight miles of the Manifold Valley between Ilam and Hulme End. The Manifold has a remarkable feature: between Wetton Mill and Ilam Hall it disappears underground, leaving its upper bed quite dry except in very wet seasons. The sceptical Dr. Johnson had to be convinced of the report by an experiment with corks that it really was the same river which emerged!

Dovedale has numerous literary associations. Dr. Johnson, Byron, Tennyson and Ruskin all praised its scenery with enthusiasm. Its closest and most productive association was with Izaak Walton and Charles Cotton, authors of that genial seventeenth-century classic, *The Compleat Angler*. Beresford Hall, which overlooked the Dove in Beresford Dale, was Cotton's birthplace and home, and Walton often visited him there. The hall is now in ruins, but the Fishing Temple which the friends used is still to be seen. The reputation of the Dove as an angler's river, and particularly as a river for trout fishing, has lasted from their day to ours. Most of the well-known hotels of the neighbourhood have angling facilities available for guests. Whether one's particular favour lies in the gentle art of fly-fishing, or merely absorbing magnificent scenic beauty without any other objectives, the attractions of Dovedale are irresistible.

Hartington is a most useful centre for exploring the upper reaches of the Dove. Footpaths run close by the stream; and the area between Hartington and the

Footbridge at the end of Wolfscote Dale

source of the river on Axe Edge well merits two or three days of delightful tramping in an air that is noted for its bracing qualities. But the better known Dovedale runs south from Hartington. A few yards from the Charles Cotton Hotel, an easy footpath leads into Beresford Dale, and then follows the river through a succession of dales to the Thorpe Cloud stepping stones. Access is also possible from a track opposite the gates of Hartington Hall, the fine seventeenth-century Manor House which is now a well-known Youth Hostel.

The public footpath runs near to the Charles Cotton Fishing Temple at the point of access to the woods. The building and estate are privately owned and not open to the public. Just beyond is the rustic bridge over the stream at the well-known and picturesque Pike Pool (mentioned in *The Compleat Angler*). This dale ends at a gap in the wall and another wooden bridge and stepping stones. Across a low-lying meadow is seen the packhorse bridge which marks the beginning of Wolfscote Dale. Paths across the bridge lead to Alstonfield and Wetton.

The Dovedale Sheepdog Trials, held in a field near the Izaak Walton Hotel and below Bunster, take place on the Tuesday and Wednesday of the third week in August each year.

The Dove Holes in Dovedale

DOVEHOLES *Map D.2*

LITTLE is left of the great Stone Circle here, its stones having been used for building purposes some 200 years ago, but Doveholes still remains of great historic interest, pre-Roman in fact, and is worth visiting from an archaeological point of view.

DOVERIDGE *Map L.3*

A VILLAGE on the Derbyshire side of the Dove between Uttoxeter and Sudbury. The church, dedicated to St. Cuthbert, stands in the grounds of Doveridge Hall (now demolished) and has a twelfth/thirteenth-century tower, a wide thirteenth-century chancel, and good fourteenth-century windows in the aisles. Doveridge was once the seat of the Lords Waterpark, a branch of the Cavendish family descended from a natural son of the 3rd Duke of Devonshire. The Doveridge Yew is remarkable but also noteworthy is the timber-framed Old Hall in the village.

DRAKELOW *Map O.5*

ATTACHED to this village 1½ miles south-west of Burton-on-Trent, was Drakelow Hall and its park, seat of the Gresley family since just after the Norman Conquest. The house was demolished in 1934 and much of the park is now occupied by Drakelow Power Station. Only the late 17th century gate piers remain.

DRAYCOTT AND CHURCH WILNE
Map M.8

DESPITE the fact that the church of St. Chad at Wilne, a very old-established one, was at one time completely destroyed by fire, the register, which dates from 1540, is in a good state of preservation and contains the record of its many associations. The font, one of the oldest in the country, is constructed from a pre-Norman cross shaft turned upside down. The effigies in the church commemorate members of the Willoughby family, and there is some good Renaissance glass.

DRONFIELD *Map D.7*

DRONFIELD is a rapidly expanding and progressive township midway between Sheffield and Chesterfield. It stands amidst hills and moorlands, and is within easy reach of the High Peak. It possesses an interesting blend of old and modern buildings, including several fine old stone houses.

The parish church of St. John the Baptist is a good example of early Gothic architecture. The tower and the nave arcades date back to the fourteenth century and the chancel, of the same period, is generally regarded as one of the most elegant in the county. Its windows contain a great wealth of ancient glass, much of it as old as the stonework which surrounds it. There are three striking roundels depicting medieval musicians.

The old Lady Chapel of the church was sacked in the reign of Henry VIII, and was restored soon after the First World War.

There is a magnificent Jacobean pulpit and the bench-ends of the choir stalls are believed to be 500 years old. Below the tower arch is a fine oak screen, and the altar table, a modern masterpiece by the famous Tideswell craftsman, Advent Hunstone, is strikingly carved. Hunstone was also responsible for the figures of Christ and the four Evangelists in canopied niches on the reredos. On the chancel floor are brass memorials to Thomas and Richard Gomfrey, two fourteenth-century priests, and there is the fine alabaster tomb of Sir Richard Barley, a fifteenth-century squire of Dronfield Woodhouse.

A Recreation Centre provides facilities for swimming (including a learners' pool), squash, badminton, table tennis, and other indoor sports, together with a sauna suite, cafeteria and bar. The Centre is an integral part of the Town Centre Development, which includes a shopping precinct with adequate provisions for car parking.

One of the major developments is within the Gosforth Valley and twelve acres of this land is currently laid out in use as public open space. Sporting facilities are available out of school hours at the Gosforth School. See also *Coal Aston*. The golf course above the town centres upon 17th century Hallowes Hall.

DUFFIELD *Map K.7*
THOUGH THE A6 ploughs slap through it, this old village has much to commend it. There are numerous quiet backwaters and many fine Georgian and Victorian houses.

It is every estate agents' idea of a favoured residential area. Even the dead are decently accommodated in the fine Victorian cemetery.

There may have been a Roman settlement here at the junction of the Derwent and the Ecclesbourne. By Norman times, certainly, its importance was considerable as the main approach to Duffield Frith, a Royal Forest some 30 miles in circumference, well stocked with deer.

The Frith was one of the many grants of the Conqueror to Henry de Ferrers, who as Earl of Derby built a considerable castle on the mound now known as Castle Hill. Excavations carried out by the Derbyshire Archaeological Society in 1886 uncovered the foundations of a massive keep with a forebuilding. The keep's outer measurements are 95 feet by 93 feet and the walls are 15 feet thick in places. Only the keeps of Dover Castle and Windsor Castle are larger. It is believed that it was from this fortress – which may have replaced a Saxon armed camp – that the Derbyshire men went to defeat the Scots at Northallerton in 1138.

But the next century saw the end of the castle. Robert de Ferrers, who with Simon de Montfort rebelled against Henry III, was badly defeated. He was pardoned, but was concerned in a second plot and was this time dispossessed of his lands and the castle destroyed by a Royalist force. The Frith passed to the Earl of Lancaster and became a royal possession in 1399. It gradually dwindled in importance, though it remained a royal preserve until the reign of Charles I.

St. Alkmund's Church contains architecture of the twelfth-fifteenth centuries. In the chapel, on a fine alabaster tomb, are the effigies of Sir Roger Mynors and his wife (1536). Sir Roger was a Sergeant in the household of Henry VII. Particularly interesting is the carved wall monument to Anthony Bradshaw, deputy steward of Duffield Frith, his two wives and twenty children. It was erected in 1600 and contains a rhyming acrostic on the name of Anthony as an epitaph. He was a great uncle of Judge John Bradshaw, who presided at the trial of Charles I, and founded an almshouse at Duffield which was pulled down in the last century.

Duffield Hall has been converted into the head-quarters of the Derbyshire Building Society. Duffield is largely residential, though there are important timber yards here and a colour works established well over 100 years ago on the site of one of the two 'Mills' mentioned in Domesday Book. Duffield Park and Tamworth House are fine buildings in this village.

EARL STERNDALE *Map F.3*
JUDGED BY the large number of ancient cairns, caves and barrows on the hills hereabouts, Earl Sterndale must have been a favoured centre in pre-historic days. The district is picturesque, with magnificent hill scenery. In Norman days it was a chapelry of Hartington, but during the eighteenth-century the fabric fell into ruin. The present church was built in 1828. The old inn has a curious sign of a headless figure, and bears the name 'Quiet Woman'!

EAST MIDLANDS INTERNATIONAL AIRPORT *Map M.8 – see also under Castle Donington.*
EAST MIDLANDS International Airport is England's third largest regional airport and lies nine miles east of Derby. It is the base for Britain's domestic airline, British Midlands; Europe's largest pure freight airline, Air Bridge Carriers; one of the world's finest aircraft completion centres, Field Aircraft, and the Recruitment and Training Centre for Britannia Airlines. The airport is next to Junction 24 on the M1, close to the new Hilton National Hotel.

ECKINGTON *Map D.8*
SITUATED TO the south of Sheffield, Eckington also embraces the villages of Renishaw, Marsh Lane and Ridgeway. Long associated with the Sitwell family, whose family seat is Renishaw Hall (*vide* Sir George Sitwell's *Tales of My Native Village*), Eckington has an exceptionally interesting church, St. Peter and Paul, which is of the twelfth-thirteenth century, in which there is an altar painting attributed to Carracci and some unusual monuments. Nearby is Mosborough Hall (now a restaurant) and a late Georgian rectory.

Recent modernisation includes a civic hall and new shopping, swimming and medical facilities. See also *Renishaw*.

EDALE *Map C.3*
EDALE MOOR, Kinder Scout and the other high altitudes of the Peak District are best observed and attacked from a base at Edale. The present church is the third built upon the site; the register dates from 1633, when a chapel was built by the people of Edale to avoid the long walk over Mam Tor to the parish church at Castleton.

The Vale of Edale is a charming, unspoiled area with a special appeal to walkers and climbers. Great cloughs cut into the Kinder hills and moors, each with its own stream and varied crags and cliffs. Crowden Head (2,070 feet) is the highest point visible from Edale, and around the Valley are Lose Hill, Win Hill (with its Roman road and Hope Cross – a pillar of stone, dated 1737), Mam Tor, Rushup Edge, Mount Famine, and others.

Nearby is Grindsbrook Font, closely resembling a cromlech, standing in a valley running through a clough in Mam Tor. From this point can be seen the track which Highland drovers followed to evade

Edale

payment of the tolls to which they would have been liable on other routes.

Hamlets of small stone houses usually bearing the name of 'Booth' (Upper Booth, Barber Booth, etc.), are dotted about the vale, and delightful footpaths can be found in almost every direction. The high, wild and magnificent plateau of Kinder, the highest place in Derbyshire, may be reached by the path up 'Jacob's Ladder' over a shoulder of Kinder, past Edale Cross (dated 1610) to Hayfield, with distant views of the famous 'Downfall' (best seen as the wind blows the falling water back on to the cliffs in streaming clouds). The 'Mermaid's Pool', just below the Downfall, is the subject of much local legend, and here Mrs. Humphry Ward placed the early scenes of her history, *David Grieve*. The Kinder path continues up William Clough, a wild water cleft, to the head of the Ashop and along the stream to the Glossop road, near the Snake Inn. The white hares of Kinder may be seen scampering on the steep hillsides in winter. The Pennine Way, a route from the Pennines to the Cheviots, commences here at Edale, from the north-east, below Grindslow Knoll.

Some of the grouse moors are closed to the public during the grouse-shooting season.

EDENSOR *Map F.5*

THIS WAS once a larger, rather untidy place, removed to its present site in 1839 by the 6th Duke of Devonshire who considered it unworthy of his otherwise well-run estate. It was rebuilt as a model village mainly for Chatsworth estate workers – laid out by Sir Joseph Paxton with houses designed in a variety of styles by himself and a Derby architect called John Robertson. On the other side of the road is the former Edensor Inn, a superb building designed by Joseph Pickford of Derby c. 1778 and now the Chatsworth Estate Office.

The church survived but was replaced some thirty years later by a large new building designed by Sir

Edensor Church

House in Edensor village

Gilbert Scott. Relics of the old church remain, notably one of the finest monuments in the county – that to Bess of Hardwick's sons Henry and William Cavendish. Lord Frederick Cavendish, murdered by the Irish in Phoenix Park, Dublin in 1882, lies here. The registers date from 1540.

In the churchyard later members of the Devonshire family are buried including the 6th Duke and his head gardener Sir Joseph Paxton. Not far away lies Kathleen Kennedy, sister of President John F. Kennedy and widow of the 10th Duke's elder son the Marquess of Hartington, killed in action in 1944. The village is pronounced 'Enzer'.

EDLASTON *Map K.4*

LYING JUST off the Derby-Ashbourne road, Edlaston is a small village close to Osmaston Park. The small church of St. James has a pretty bell-cote with two bells hanging exposed, and a fourteenth-century chancel.

EDNASTON *Map K.5*

A VILLAGE close to the Derby-Ashbourne road with an ancient hostelry named after a huge yew tree. Ednaston Manor, though no longer the home of the Player family for whom it was built to the designs of Sir Edwin Lutyens, is still a private house and the famous gardens though closed at the time of writing may be open to the public again.

EGGINTON *Map M.5*

A QUIET village on the Dove, 8 miles south-west of Derby and 4 miles north of Burton upon Trent, with the fourteenth-century Monk's Bridge, so called after its repair by the Abbot of Burton. Records say that the church bells were sold to repair the bridge, 'which is so farre in decay that the township is not able to mend the same'. Egginton Hall, the magnificent seat of the Every family, was demolished after World War II but the family, whose monuments can be seen in the 14th century church, still lives in the village.

ELDON HOLE *Map D.3*

THE REMARKABLE swallet pit at the base of Eldon Hill called 'Eldon Hole' is an unusually large cavity, descended only by rope ladders, nearly 200 feet deep, the bottomless pit of ancient tradition, with further caverns going to a greater depth. It can be reached only on foot from Castleton or Peak Forest.

ELMTON *Map E.9*

THE CHURCH is of 18th century design with an unusual stunted west tower capped by a low gable roof. It is built on the site of an earlier building as the registers date from 1559. Inside there is an excellent 18th century carved pulpit and tester. Nearby is Markland Grips, a gorge-like natural feature which is the site of an ancient promontory fort.

ELTON *Map G.5*

ASSOCIATED WITH lead-mining, a feature of the countryside surrounding this small village is the close pattern of stone farm buildings and fields. The church, which dates from 1812, replaces a much earlier building destroyed when the spire collapsed in the 1800s.

ELVASTON *Map M.8*

A PLEASANT rural village less than a mile from the A6 situated close to Elvaston Castle and its park, the seat until recent times of the Earls of Harrington. The church, close to the Castle, is well-known for its fine monuments to the Stanhope family, notably Byron's friend, the 5th Earl of Harrington who was with him in Greece.

ELVASTON CASTLE *Map M.8* see page 13.

ETWALL *Map M.5*

A LARGE village 6 miles south-west of Derby, on the main road to Uttoxeter and the Potteries. It is noted as the home of Sir John Port who founded Repton School in the sixteenth century. The church of St. Helen has Norman work in the north arcade, Early English work in the chancel and monuments to the Port family. There are signs of several restorations, however, and the church was largely rebuilt by Sir John Port following a violent storm in 1545. There is a monument here to Sir Arthur Cochrane (1872-1954), Clarenceux King-of-Arms. The Port Hospital, almshouses rebuilt in 1681 and recently restored, adjoin the churchyard.

The large John Port Comprehensive school stands in the grounds of Etwall Hall, one of Derbyshire's many fine country houses which are now no more.

EYAM *Map D.5*

WRITING IN the 1920s, H. V. Morton said 'In the quiet Derbyshire village of Eyam, men still talk about the Plague of London as though it happened last week'. It is much the same today and the main reason why people visit the place is to pay tribute in some way to a tragic story of human gallantry which will never be forgotten.

The Plague was brought from London in 1665 in a consignment of clothes resulting in the death of five out of every six inhabitants within a few months.

The church and the churchyard were closed and the dead were buried in the fields in hastily-constructed graves. Services were conducted by the Rector, the Rev. William Mompesson, who preached in a dell from a lofty rock, since called 'Cucklet Church', where an annual Commemoration Service is now held on the last Sunday in August. During the plague the inhabitants accepted a rigid routine of isolation, and purchased their supplies from neighbouring areas by depositing their 'contagious money' in a well, now called 'Mompesson's Well', after which supplies were left upon the stones in isolated spots. The rector was assisted by Thomas Stanley, the ejected dissenting minister, who had stayed on at Eyam. A well-dressing festival is held at Eyam, starting on the Saturday before Plague Sunday.

The Port Almshouses at Etwall

Eyam Church

The thirteenth-fifteenth century Church of St. Lawrence contains a Norman font and the chair of William Mompesson (1665). In the churchyard is a fine Anglian cross, probably of the ninth century, and the grave of Catherine Mompesson, the heroic rector's wife. Eyam Hall in the Derbyshire vernacular dates from 1676 and there are other old houses in the village. The beautiful rectory built for the Rev. Thomas Seward in 1768 was shamefully demolished some years ago. Seward was a friend of Dr. Johnson. His daughter, Anna, wrote poetry and was known as 'The Swan of Lichfield'.

Near the village is the 'Sir William Road', a hill

Eyam Hall and stocks

route nearly 1,200 feet above the sea from which there are magnificent views of the Peak District, with Axe Edge, Mam Tor, and Kinder Scout in the distance. 'Rock Garden', or the places of echoes, is near the village. The stone circle, the 'Wet Withins', is on Eyam Moor, surrounded by several lesser circles, and there are many barrows as yet unexplored on the Moor. 'Slickensides', a species of galena found in the local lead mines, possesses dangerous explosive properties.

The Riley Graves, where Plague victims lie buried, are on a hill outside the village.

FARNAH GREEN *Map J.6*
AS YOU drive north west from Duffield, leaving the busy A6 behind, you soon hit lovely rural Derbyshire with pheasants and squirrels scampering off the verges. Before reaching Belper is this charming hamlet of Farnah Green. It has no shops but the *Blue Bell* is a pleasant old country pub which serves food.

FENNY BENTLEY *Map J.4*
A PRETTY village 2 miles north of Ashbourne on the main Buxton road. The rebuilt church of St. Edmund has rich sixteenth century screens and a rare and curious Elizabethan alabaster monument to Thomas Beresford and his wife, Agnes, together with their 16 sons and five daughters. It takes the form of two recumbent figures completely enveloped in shrouds, with the 21 incised effigies of their children treated in a similar manner. The father and eight sons formed, together with their retainers, a complete troop of horse under Henry V and distinguished themselves at Agincourt in 1415. The seventeenth-century manor house, east of the church, has a medieval tower and was at one time the home of a branch of the Beresford family.

FINDERN *Map M.6*
THIS VILLAGE is situated just off the Derby–Burton-on-Trent road about eight miles from Derby. No trace can be found of Finderne Great House where Isabella Finderne lived five hundred years ago. All Saints Church was built in 1863 and contains the tympanum from the original Norman building.

FLAGG *Map F.3*
A HIGH-LYING hamlet midway between Chelmorton and Monyash. Flagg Hall, a picturesque Elizabethan building, contains some good oak-panelled rooms, and has associations with the Dales and Fynnes, both old Derbyshire families. The High Peak Hunt point-to-point races are held nearby.

FOOLOW *Map D.4*
THIS SMALL village might well be called typical of upland Derbyshire. Stone-built and self-contained, it can have changed little over the centuries. Three wells remind one of its past and there is a bull ring still to be seen near the village cross. St. Hugh's is a small church with an arched entrance and a single bell-tower.

FOREMARK *Map N.7*
THE CHURCH of St. Saviour, between Repton and Ingleby, is an unusual but interesting building of

Foremark Hall, former seat of the Burdett family and now a prep-school

1662 in a late-Perpendicular style retaining much of its old woodwork, including the rood screen, box pews and three-decker pulpit. The communion rails are a fine example of wrought ironwork fashioned by Robert Bakewell, the eighteenth century ironsmith, who also made the gates leading into the hall grounds.

Foremark Hall, designed by David Hiorne of Warwick (d. 1759) for Sir Robert Burdett, was completed in 1762 by Joseph Pickford as clerk-of-the-works. It is a Georgian house with a notable entrance, a lake and extensive woodlands. The Hall, for many generations the seat of the Burdett family, is now used as the preparatory department of Repton School.

FOSTON AND SCROPTON *Map M.4*

THESE TWO villages lie near to the county border close to Sudbury. Arthur Agard, the famous antiquary, buried in Westminster Abbey, was born at Foston in 1540. He was an authority on ancient manuscripts and heraldry and a founder member of the Society of Antiquaries. Foston Hall, a Victorian 'Jacobean' building, is now a house of correction. At Scropton an attractive half-timbered house stands at the confluence of the river Dove and Foston Brook. Buried in the interesting Victorian church of St. Paul is a swashbuckling Admiral – Sir Arthur Cumming who fought pirates and died in 1893.

FRITCHLEY *Map H.7*

AN INTERESTING old village on the hilly road from Ambergate to Crich that once played a strong local part in the Quaker movement (the 'Fritchley Friends').

FROGGATT *Map D.5*

THE VILLAGE of Froggatt likes between Calver and Grindleford, under Froggatt Edge and not far from White Edge. Froggatt Edge itself presents a typical Derbyshire upland scene, with its long escarpment which can be seen for miles around.

GLAPWELL *Map E.9*

ABOUT THREE miles from Bolsover, seven miles from Chesterfield Glapwell is the smallest parish in the Bolsover district.

GLOSSOP *Map B.2*

THIS DERBYSHIRE town has its roots deep in English history, possessing evidence of occupation during Roman, Saxon, Norman and medieval times. Melandra the most northerly of the three Roman forts in Derbyshire, was situated here.

Glossop Hall and much of the town was part of the estate of the Dukes of Norfolk. In the last century it became the property of Lord Edward Fitzalan-Howard, second son of the 13th Duke. He was an M.P. and Vice Chamberlain to Queen Victoria and was created Lord Howard of Glossop. His great-grandson is the 17th Duke of Norfolk.

In 1924 the estate was sold to the Town Council and is now a public park (the Hall has been demolished).

The town is now industrial and residential and surrounded by a belt of arable and pasture land to the edge of the moors. From almost every quarter wide panoramic prospects of mountains and moor are visible.

Within the boundaries of the town are good swimming facilities, four parks, six recreation grounds, first-class cricket and football grounds, and a golf course that appears to be part of the surrounding moorland. A new leisure centre with multi-purpose hall and four squash courts, was opened in 1979.

Many finely restored steam engines are kept in the new Exhibition Hall which was constructed largely by voluntary effort (the Centre is maintained by the Bahamas Locomotive Society, an educational charity) and there are also locomotives on view which are currently being renovated. From time to time some of the engines are used to haul special excursions for enthusiasts in the Derbyshire area.

The town lies on the foothills that lead to the mass of Kinder Scout, the highest point of the Peak of Derbyshire. By charming moorland paths one can quickly be in the very heart of the finest scenery – Mill Hill, Kinder Downfall, Kinder Low, Fairbrook Naze – and the moors leading towards Sheffield are easily accessible.

There is a flourishing sailing club at Torside Reservoir north of the town and Bottoms Water Park and Ski Club is a popular venue near Tintwistle.

Old Glossop, where the parish church stands, with its medieval market cross, old manor house and 17th century houses is a fascinating part of the town.

Glossop is an essential part of gritstone in England. Its moors and fells abound in the contours peculiar to this stratum. Everywhere on the hills surrounding the town are to be found crags and outcrops which provide splendid training for the enthusiast contemplating serious rock work. From Glossop as a centre one may reach out to magnificent excursions in almost every direction. There are not only the moorlands of the Peak, there are also the great moorland wilderness over Bleaklow and the Saddleworth moors stretching to Melton and Marsden. The fells around Glossop are as savage as the Yorkshire fells and are a fascination to the experienced tramper. Glossop is truly the gateway to the Peak, either by car over the rugged Snake Pass, or on foot over Doctor's Gate – an old Roman road.

GLUTTON *Map E.3*
JUST THE place for a restaurant. This curiously-named hamlet is in Glutton Dale, a pass at Park Hill in north west Derbyshire near Earl Sterndale (q.v.). Glutton Bridge crosses the Dove at the foot of the pass.

GOYT VALLEY *Map E.1*
THE LOWER part of the Goyt Valley is flooded to form a reservoir but the natural beauty of the surrounding area has been retained and there are pleasant footpaths for the walker. The Goyt rises about four miles south-west of Buxton, and discharges into the Mersey near Stockport. Throughout its course the valley is distinguished by the richness of its vegetation, the steep banks are clothed to the water's edge with woods of great variety, and it is one of the best areas for natural history.

Errwood Reservoir is situated immediately to the south of Fernilee Reservoir and has a capacity of 935 million gallons. About 1,000 yards of the Street have disappeared and a new road skirts the water, crossing Shooter's Clough a little more than half way up from the former Goyt's Bridge (which has been rebuilt elsewhere) to the ruins and romantic park of Errwood Hall. Another road crosses the top of the barrage, joining the Street on one side, and following the course of the old mineral railway up the hillside joining Goyt's Lane on the east side of the valley.

GREAT HUCKLOW *Map D.4*
A HAMLET situated near the end of Sir William Road,

on the hills above Tideswell (2 miles), once much noted for its Village Drama Players, who converted a barn into a splendidly equipped 'theatre'. Unfortunately the theatre was closed down in 1971, ironically, not for lack of audiences but of suitable actors. The Florence Nightingale Memorial Home for men and women is a holiday centre, built specially of local stone by the Unitarian Sunday School Union. Great Hucklow is the gliding centre of Derbyshire. See p. 31.

GREAT LONGSTONE *Map E.4*
THE OLD village of one long street, sheltered by the fine range of Longstone Edge, is approached from the west by an avenue of elm trees. The village cross appears to date back to an early century, when the Flemish weavers settled in this part of Derbyshire and established the stocking industry. The view from the highest point of Longstone Edge (1,300 feet) is one of the finest in the country, covering the greater part of north and west Derbyshire. The Church of St. Giles dates from the thirteenth century, with well preserved registers dating from 1638. An old building, now used as a garage, was formerly part of the house occupied by the then Earl of Shrewsbury. Great Longstone Hall is one of the most attractive of the smaller country houses in Derbyshire and one of only two in the Peak to be built of brick.

GRINDLEFORD *Map D.5*
DERBYSHIRE'S famous 'edge' and rock scenery is within easy reach from Grindleford and from the hill route, Sir William Road, there are magnificent views of the Peak and of gliding activities off Bradwell Edge. On the north is a magnificent stretch of moor and woodland. The Longshaw estate (q.v.) of 1,086 acres is one of the finest open spaces owned by the National Trust.

Padley Chapel, restored in recent times for Roman Catholic services, is one of the most interesting survivals of the fifteenth century in the county. Centuries ago it was probably part of the great hall of Padley Manor, but all that remains now of the old house are the foundations. The chapel is the scene of an annual pilgrimage to honour the memory of two Roman Catholic priests, Nicholas Garlic and Robert Ludlam, who were taken from here to Derby on 25th July, 1588, and hanged, drawn and quartered. The ceremony is on Thursday nearest July 12th. See page 28.

GRINDLOW *Map D.4*
CLOSE TO Great Hucklow, Grindlow was an ancient settlement and has an interesting prehistoric round barrow.

HADDON HALL *Map F.5 see page 14.*

HADFIELD *Map A.1*
ON THE very edge of the county, Hadfield lies at the tip of the Longdendale watershed in an area of spectacular walks and tours. It has St. Andrew's Church built in 1874 and a Roman Catholic church of slightly earlier date. The oldest building is the Old Hall dated 1646.

HANBURY *Map M.4*
A SMALL hill village (in Staffordshire), the site of an

Anglo-Saxon monastery of the seventh century, where St. Werburga, a daughter of King Wulfere, was abbess. The present church, much restored, is an Anglo-Saxon foundation, and traces of earth fortifications are to be found in the district, along with alabaster workings.

HANDLEY *Map D.8*
IN REALITY three hamlets – West, Middle, and Nether Handley, all close to Staveley and fairly rural in spite of that. A very charming Victorian church serves this scattered community.

HANGING BRIDGE *Map J.4*
HANGING BRIDGE, over the Dove on the Ashbourne-Mayfield road, was until 1887 in the parish of Offcote but is now in the parish of Clifton. Situated in a very fine section of the border country, it is the haunt of fishermen. The River Dove at this point reaches its greatest width.

HARBOROUGH ROCKS *Map J.5*
A WILD and mysterious outcrop of limestone near Brassington weathered into eerie shapes. A cave was occupied by humans in the early Iron Age but who carved the great stone throne? Was it made from the action of the wind or was it hewn for some ancient barbaric chieftain to sit in and hold council with his tribe? It might even be the whim of some 18th century antiquary.

Another mystery is the hollowed-out 'font' complete with plug-hole. Was this an early Christian site also? We can only guess as we stand on this windswept height 1,200 feet above sea level and survey the wide views.

HARDWICK HALL *Map G.9* see page 16.

HARTINGTON *Map G.3*
THE SCENERY around this attractive village close to Dovedale, especially the fine limestone hills which flank the river, attracts a large number of people. Nearby are the ruins of Beresford Hall, Charles Cotton's birthplace and home, and Beresford Dale is reached by a short footpath from the village. The path alongside the Dove can be followed right through to Ashbourne.

Hartington Hall, which dates from 1350 (rebuilt in 1611) is now a Youth Hostel. St. Giles' Church is an

Hartington village

interesting building of the thirteenth century, with many fine monuments and curious gargoyles.

One of the secondary titles of the Dukes of Devonshire is Marquess of Hartington, used as a courtesy title by the eldest son and heir.

HARTSHORNE *Map O.6*
THIS VILLAGE, near Swadlincote, has an ancient church (St. Peter) which dates from the fourteenth century, though there was an almost complete rebuilding in 1835; it contains alabaster effigies of Humphrey Dethick and his wife (1599). Several pleasant old farmhouses survive in spite of encroaching urbanisation. Next to the church is the Upper Hall, a 17th century timber-framed building.

HASSOP *Map E.5*
A CHARMING unspoiled village 2½ miles from Bakewell. Hassop Hall, now an hotel, is a mainly seventeenth century building and former seat of the Eyres of Hassop later claimants to the earldom of Newburgh. Latterly it belonged to the Stephenson family. The Classical Revival Etruscan style Church of All Saints was built by the Roman Catholic Eyres in 1816.

HATHERSAGE *Map D.5*
A VILLAGE redolent of literary associations and legend. Its fine church stands high above the houses

Hathersage

and has a collection of brasses to the Eyre family which once owned several houses in the vicinity –

North Lees Hall, Hathersage

87

Highlow Hall, Brookfield Hall, North Lees Hall (attributed to Robert Smythson), Moorseats Hall and Offerton Hall. Although the family has long since lapsed into obscurity, their name has been immortalised by Charlotte Brontë who came here to see her friend Ellen Nussey whose brother was the Vicar. She took the name for the heroine of her book *Jane Eyre*. It is said that Charlotte also stayed at the George Hotel, Hathersage where a room and a desk are preserved.

In the churchyard is an inordinately long grave, reputedly that of Little John. There is a fine Hall at the east end of the Village and the Victorian Nether Hall is to the South.

HATTON *Map M.4*
HATTON lies just off the main Derby-Uttoxeter road. Beyond the Dove are the remains of Tutbury Castle. A modern secondary and primary modern school is situated at Hatton.

HAYFIELD *Map C.2*
IN THE highest section of the Peak District, Hayfield is a popular gateway to Kinder Scout. The church of St. Matthew was rebuilt in 1386, and again in 1818 with the addition of a new tower in 1894. In the crypt, below the present flooring, may be seen the bases of the pillars of two ancient arcades.

Throughout the year the village attracts large numbers of visitors from the Manchester district, who take great delight in the fine moorlands and valleys surrounding it. Most of the ways for the approach to the Kinder plateau branch from the road at the rear of the Royal Hotel where John Wesley stayed in 1755 when he visited Hayfield to preach. The old fair at Hayfield prompted the writing of *Come Lassies and Lads*. The late Arthur Lowe, the actor, was born here.

HAZELWOOD *Map J.6*
PRIMARILY A residential place without much semblance of being a village. There are a number of fine houses but the little church of 1840 is on its own forming a group with school and vicarage of the same date. The church is unusual in having a clock over the entrance porch. It stands in a charming churchyard and is approached by a short tree-lined drive.

HEAGE *Map J.7*
BETWEEN Ripley, Ambergate and Belper are scattered the farms and houses of Heage. From the higher points views of the Cromford Canal and the Amber Valley can be had. Heage Hall, in Nether Heage, was the home of a branch of the Pole family for centuries. Heage Windmill, which is one of the best examples of a tower mill in the county, with the usual number of six sails, has been restored.

HEANOR *Map J.8*
HEANOR, which includes Langley Mill, Codnor and Loscoe (q.v.) is a town of considerable importance with a wide and growing range of industries. Its growth from a village dates from the first Industrial Revolution which brought the canals and then the railways, and its future is assured by the closeness of the M1 Motorway. Industrial development is actively encouraged, several of the large old established firms

D. H. Lawrence, whose house at Eastwood is now a museum

have been greatly modernising and extending their premises and many new enterprises have been started in and close to the town. Coal mining, the former staple industry, has moved out of the district with the closing of the last operating colliery. Much attention is being given to the landscaping of damaged land in order to restore fully the considerable attractions of the neighbourhood: one former colliery at Loscoe has been transformed into playing fields and another at Langley is planned for reclamation as a site for open space, residential and industrial development. A reclaimed worked opencast site, together with the parkland woods, hills and lakes of the former Shipley Hall (q.v.) are now a pleasant Country Park. Here also is The American Adventure (see page 6).

A modern covered swimming pool and learners' pool are situated adjacent to the Memorial Park.

D. H. Lawrence, the novelist, was born and grew to manhood two miles away at Eastwood and his accurate and sympathetic descriptions of the locality have done much to renew public appreciation of its beauties. These were also well appreciated in earlier times by the well-known Victorian novelists and poets William and Mary Howitt who were closely connected with Heanor.

The ancient Parish Church of St. Lawrence, rebuilt in 1868, contained many twelfth century details of which today only a remnant survives, but the fifteenth century west tower is still intact.

HEATH *Map F.8*
A PLEASANT agricultural village, referred to in Domesday Book as the Two Lunts and later as Lound or Heath, the former name persisting in open field names. Here are the seventeenth century remains of a Norman church latterly a mortuary chapel but now a ruin.

Stone carvings believed to be pre-Norman can be

found in the porch of the present church which was built in 1852 and dedicated to All Saints.

Remains of ancient earthworks lie to the South West of the village. The one remaining thatched cottage, cruck built, is the site of the village well-dressing held annually in July. There is an access point to the M1 motorway near the village.

HIGH PEAK TRAIL see under Tissington.

HIGHAM *Map G.8*
HIGHAM WAS part of the Ogston Hall estate and is now in a conservation area. Ogston Reservoir is in the vicinity. The village contains many excellent 17th century houses. There are still folk memories of the ox-roastings which took place to celebrate George III's jubilee in 1810 and later the victory of Waterloo. Today the village is also notable for its fine inns. Its history goes back to remote times as it straddles the old Roman road (Ryknield Street) between Derby and Chesterfield.

Ogston Hall, formerly seat of the Turbutt family, now belongs to the Wakefields who have restored it.

HILTON *Map M.5*
HILTON, ON THE main Derby-Uttoxeter road, is a village of some importance with large gravel works. It is situated within a short walk of a pretty stretch of the Dove past Marston's thirteenth century church, surrounded by lawns and containing Derbyshire's oldest bell, cast by John de Stafford of Leicester in 1360.

In Hilton itself is a fine old half-timbered house said by tradition to have been a seat of the Wakelyn family in the 17th century. It later became an inn and a posting house.

HINDLOW *Map F.3*
JUST OFF the main Ashbourne-Buxton road, to the west and about three miles short of Buxton lies Hindlow. Its railway station, now closed to normal passenger trains, is a relic of the 19th-century railway boom.

HOB TOR *Map D.2*
ON HIGH ground (1,644 ft), Hob Tor offers good walking and climbing facilities for the hardy.

HOGNASTON *Map J.5*
BUILT ON a hill climbing to the Ashbourne road, Hognaston village is little known but well worth a visit. The church is of particular interest being partly thirteenth century (the 5-foot walls of the tower) and partly fifteenth century (the belfry with its pinnacles and gargoyles). In the Norman porch are carvings and an ancient oak door. Hognaston Winn rises nearly 1,000 feet high and overlooks the village.

HOLBROOK *Map K.7*
LIKE HORSLEY (q.v.) this is a surprising oasis close to Derby with attractive old houses and some modern housing development. The church of 1841 is pure Georgian in spirit of plain classical design. This is perhaps because it is a rebuild of a predecessor built in 1761. On higher ground behind the churchyard, which has some interesting tombstones, is Holbrook Hall (1681 but looks later). Southwood House is another handsome residence, built by the Bourne family who owned Denby Pottery in the 1880s.

HOLLINGTON *Map L.5*
A PLEASANT village in a farming area close to which runs the Shirley Brook, to the west, and Brailsford Brook to the east.

HOLLOWAY see under Dethick.

HOLMESFIELD *Map D.6*
AN ANCIENT manor on the hills south-west of Sheffield, given by Edward VI to 'his trusty friend and counsellor, Sir William de Cavendish'. At the time of the Domesday the manor was in the hands of the Deincourts. Holmesfield is situated amid fine moorland scenery, and the Barlow Foxhounds have kennels in the parish. The fine 17th century Hall has been restored.

HOLYMOORSIDE *Map F.7*
THIS MOORLAND area, close to Chesterfield on the western side, rises in parts to over 1,000 feet and is skirted by East Moor and on to the grounds of Chatsworth.

HOPE *Map C.4*
IN THE CENTRE of the Hope Valley, on the Peakshole Water and Noe River, adjacent to Castleton, Hathersage, Bamford, and the district leading towards the Peak and Kinder Scout. The Church of St. Peter, by the side of the road near the Noe, is almost surrounded by sycamore and lime trees. It has a squat west tower showing some Early English features and is remarkable also for its large uncouth gargoyles. The rebuilt chancel contains fourteenth century sedilia and thirteenth century piscina; and in the churchyard is the shaft of a Saxon cross.

Fishing and rough shooting may be enjoyed in this area, which offers many delightful walks and excursions. Within easy reach is the famous Mam Tor or 'Shivering Mountain'. Wells are dressed at Hope, on the nearest Saturday to St. Peter's Day, and the ceremony usually begins the Hope Wakes Week. The Hope Valley Agricultural Show and Sheep Dog Trials, held on August Bank Holiday, attract a great deal of attention. Hope Valley College is one of the first of the rural centres for higher education.

HOPTON *Map H.5*
HOPTON SHARES the church at Carsington (q.v.) the next-door village. The main building here is Hopton Hall which hides behind a crinkle-crankle wall and for many centuries was the seat of the Gell family who claim a Roman descent. The house is basically Elizabethan with many eighteenth century additions. In Elizabethan times Anthony Gell founded the school and almshouses which still bear his name at Wirksworth and is buried in the church there. Sir John Gell was a Parliamentary general in the Civil War and his portrait and several personal possessions were preserved in the Hall. His descendant, Sir William Gell, was a classical scholar, traveller and friend of Sir Walter Scott. Philip Gell built the Via Gellia (q.v.) in the eighteenth century. The Hall was sold by the Gells in 1989 but is still a private residence.

Townend House has an intriguing piece of Saxon carving let into the outside wall and the almshouses were built by Sir Philip Gell between 1719 and 1722.

Hopton Stone takes its name from Hopton Wood quarries which lie a little to the north east of the village between Wirksworth and Middleton.

HORSLEY *Map K.7*
APPROACHED FROM the bottom of the hill, this seems a remarkable place so close to Derby and surrounded by busy roads yet its core is tranquil, its buildings pleasant. At the end of a short *cul-de-sac* is a real gem – the 14th century church with its broach spire and mid-15th century battlements standing amid a profusion of tombstones and rose-beds – from the outside surely one of the most attractive village churches in the County. Inside it has been much restored. In one window are small fragments of very early glass.

Only a few vestiges remain of Horsley Castle, once a huge Norman stronghold. The other end of the village turns into anonymous suburbia with hanging name-signs, 'ranch' fencing, etc.

HUCKLOW — See under Great Hucklow, Little Hucklow.

HULLAND and HULLAND WARD
Map J.5
ON HIGH ground, from which fine views covering many miles can be had, these neighbouring villages lie on the Ashbourne-Belper road, which further on passes through Turnditch and Shottlegate. Hulland Hall (1770s) and the Old Hall (17th century) are notable buildings.

HUNGRY BENTLEY *Map L.4*
THE VILLAGE (one mile east of Cubley) no longer exists though the old street patterns can still be discerned in surrounding fields. Part of Bentley Hall is all that survives, a splendid Jacobean wing with a stylish brick addition of c.1670. Cf. Alkmonton.

HURDLOW *Map F.3*
A HAMLET situated on the Bakewell to Leek road, close to the straight Roman road section of the Ashbourne to Buxton road. It is a favourite locality for walkers and there is accommodation for visitors.

IBLE *Map H.5*
JUST A few scattered farms remote from the madding crowd, this hamlet is isolated on high ground not far from Middleton-by-Wirksworth where D. H. Lawrence lived for a time. His story 'Wintry Peacock' is set in Ible.

IDRIDGEHAY *Map J.6*
SOMETIMES CALLED 'Ithersee' by the locals, this is a small village in the Ecclesbourne Valley with shop, flower-decked houses, a pub with Gothick windows and an attractive early station now converted to a private house. The fine church of St. James was designed by Stephens in 1854 and South Sitch is a half-timbered house which looks more like a building in Warwickshire than the home of a minor 17th century Derbyshire gentleman. It contains a medieval hall house.

ILAM (Staffordshire) *Map J.3*
A MODEL village one mile from Thorpe. The Gothic cross in the centre of the village was erected in memory of Mrs. Watts-Russell, who formerly lived at Ilam Hall which was presented to the National Trust in 1934 as a Youth Hostel by Sir Robert McDougall. The Hall is still an imposing and stately structure, though a substantial part of it was demolished when it became a youth hostel. The Church, which stands in the grounds of the Hall, is of Norman origin, but like the Hall was rebuilt during the 19th century. Some Norman parts of it remain, and it contains a highly elaborate monument by Chantrey depicting the death-bed scene of David Pike Watts, surrounded by his only daughter and her children. Other memorials include the altar tomb of Robert Meverell (d. 1625) of Throwley Hall (the ruins of which are nearby), whose daughter married Thomas, Lord Cromwell. In the churchyard are the remains of pre-Norman shafts and crosses. Also in the grounds of Ilam Hall is the ancient shrine of St. Bertram who is reputed to have lived as a hermit in these parts in Anglo-Saxon times and to have converted the district to Christianity.

Chantrey's striking monument of the death-bed scene of David Pike Watts in Ilam Church

Ilam is a natural starting point for exploring the Manifold Valley; there is a fine stretch of the Manifold in the grounds of the Hall where, beneath the cliffs, the river regains its overland course after the subterranean journey from higher upstream. The river between Wetton Mill and Ilam, which are nearly four miles apart, has two courses – one above ground, which is sometimes dry, and the other below, through an underground lake. Near the river is the yew-shaded grotto in the cliff where the witty seventeenth century dramatist, William Congreve, wrote his comedy *The Old Bachelor*.

Ilam is a pretty, unspoiled village and very popular with ramblers. The Dovedale Sheep Dog Trials are held here in August. There is excellent accommodation for visitors at the nearby Izaak Walton Hotel, which has local fishing rights. Not far away is Castern Hall the charming home of the Hurt family.

ILKESTON *Map K.9*

THE THIRD largest town in Derbyshire stands on high ground above the Erewash Valley on the eastern border of the county. It is 9½ miles north-east of Derby and 7½ miles north-west of Nottingham. Known as Tilchestune in the Domesday Book, Ilkeston's first charter for a weekly market (now held on Thursdays and Saturdays) and for an annual fair (now held on three days in October) was granted in 1252, and the town became a Municipal Borough by royal charter in 1887.

Ilkeston's parish church of St. Mary was in existence at least in the twelfth century but is now almost entirely Victorian restoration work, mainly in

Ilkeston Church. Below: crusading knight – Sir Nicholas de Cantelupe (d. 1272)

the Decorated style, carried out in 1855, but it does still contain some thirteenth century work and has some seventeenth century bells. The tower was completely dismantled in 1910 and re-erected further west to allow extensions to be made to the nave. One of the monuments is the tomb of Nicholas de Cantelupe, whose family were lords of the manor in the thirteenth century. One of their number was St. Thomas of Hereford.

Another building of historic interest is the Old Hall at Little Hallam, about half a mile south of the Market Place. This is a fine example of Jacobean half-timbered work with traces of an older, stone-built structure at ground level and below. A few yards away, on Little Hallam Hill, stands 'The Gables', which is probably eighteenth century or even late seventeenth in origin. Ball's Factory in Burr Lane is a good example of early industrial architecture. The base of the medieval market cross now stands in the Garden of Remembrance, which itself was provided by public subscription after the 1939-45 war in the Parish Churchyard facing the Market Place.

Iron and concrete products, engineering, hosiery, lingerie, lace and fabrics are the basic industries, but there are also plastics, bedding, knitwear, packaging, food distribution, clothing, electrical goods, electronics and a variety of small industries. The coal mines have gone and more than one site has been turned into a recreation ground or playing field.

The Erewash Valley Golf Club has an 18-hole course just south of the town and the Rutland Recreation Ground is the scene of many a local cricket match. Ilkeston Round Table has provided a children's paddling pool at the ground. Midland League football is provided on the Manor Ground by Ilkeston Town Football Club, and rugby football at Gallows Inn Playing Fields by Ilkeston Rugby Union Football Club. The Borough Council has a nine-hole municipal golf course at Pewit, which is to be extended to eighteen holes. An indoor swimming complex known as the Victoria Park Leisure Centre is situated in Manners Road and there is a ten-pin Bowling Centre in Derby Road.

In 1957, Ilkeston and Chalons-sur-Marne in the Champagne district of France became 'twin towns'.

INGLEBY *Map N.7*

TRENTSIDE HAMLET with a curious Anchorite cave. Close by is Sevenspouts Hill, which has a striking view.

The little hamlet contains a number of charming old cottages and the water supply springs from rocks rising above the winding lane in front of them. The neighbourhood is rich in timber and there are many enchanting woodland and riverside walks – including the quiet byway which links the hamlet with Swarkestone Bridge. There is a pagan Danish cemetery in Heath Wood, containing 50 graves.

KEDLESTON HALL *Map L.6* see p. 18.

KELSTEDGE *Map F.7*

A SMALL HAMLET with a pleasant inn situated four miles north east of Matlock on the A632.

KILBURN *Map J.7*

KILBURN, two miles south of Denby, is a fairly large village with much new development. Its chief building is the Hall, a fine building, largely Jacobean, with gables.

KINDER SCOUT *Map B.2*

KINDER SCOUT is a wild and barren plateau, with rugged rock formations characteristic of this part of the Peak District National Park. A large area of the Kinder plateau, previously debarred to walkers, is

Kinder Scout and Fairbrook

now available to ramblers through access agreements concluded with several landowners. Still strictly preserved as grouse moors, parts of the 'new' areas are closed to visitors each year on 12th August and certain subsequent days during August, September and October. Information may be obtained locally from the National Park Information Centre at Fieldhead, Edale.

The chief elevations of Kinder Scout are: Kinder Low, 2,088 feet; Fairbrook Naze, 2,049 feet; and Crowden Head, 2,070 feet. The mountain valleys – cloughs, as they are known locally – are very beautiful. The Downfall, especially after a copious rainfall, is a magnificent sight. The 'Mermaid's Pool' just below is the subject of much local legend. The footpath from Edale via Jacob's Ladder to Hayfield and thence by William Clough to the famous Snake Inn is very popular. Good hotel and other accommodation can be found here and at Edale and Hayfield.

KING'S NEWTON *Map N.8*
NOT A brick out of place in this village of near perfect

harmony. The 17th century Hall of the Hardinge family was burnt out in 1859 and remained a forlorn shell until the railway magnate Sir Cecil Paget restored it in 1910. The old village cross is now in Melbourne church and was replaced in 1936 with another which has the distinction of marking the accession of Edward VIII and must be a rare object, if not unique.

The Derbyshire naturalist and antiquarian John Briggs lived in this village. The Hardinge Arms and the Packhorse are fine buildings and popular public houses.

KING STERNDALE *Map E.3*
THREE MILES from Buxton this village extends along the southern bank of the river Wye. Wye Dale, Ashwood Dale and Deep Dale, are easily accessible. Deep Dale, a limestone ravine, is reached from the main road about half a mile past the turning to King Sterndale village. Black Dale and Horseshoe Dale,

The main street of King's Newton showing the 17th century Chantry House (centre left)

two small ravines at the head of Deep Dale, can also be reached from the Ashbourne-Buxton road. These dales can only be traversed on foot..

KIRK HALLAM *Map K.9*

PART OF the town of Ilkeston, here is a lovely old church, and a local history going back to Saxon days, but with substantial modern housing development.

KIRK IRETON *Map J.5*

AN OLD-WORLD village overlooking the Ecclesbourne Valley about mid-way between Ashbourne and Wirksworth. It has good examples of old domestic architecture and a church with remains of Norman construction. The nave arcades have a special charm and there is delicate work of the fourteenth century.

The 'Barley Mow' is one of the very few remaining real old English pubs unsullied by the chromium taste of the breweries and innocent of canned 'music' and the accursed 'space invaders'. It serves real ale and is a memorable place.

KIRK LANGLEY *Map L.6*

A VILLAGE on the Derby-Ashbourne road. The Church of St. Michael is mainly a structure of the fourteenth century, with a later tower. The interior has a numinous charm of quite exceptional character. The lover of handicrafts will be interested in the remains of ancient woodwork, especially the screen enclosing the Meynell Choir which contains fine work of the fifteenth century. Other ancient screenwork endorses the entrance vestibule at the west door and in the south choir chapel the east window contains Flemish glass (four lights) dated 1631, and signed Jane Seye. The north aisle contains other Flemish glass, as well as a war memorial window. Beautifully executed modern panelling is seen in the choir and elsewhere. The Meynell family (*vide* Meynell Langley) held land here as early as the reign of Henry I. The Poles of Radbourne also had interests here, and there is a large marble altar-tomb commemorating Henry Pole and his wife (1558).

KNIVETON *Map J.5*

AMONG WINDING lanes in a dip stands this village, 2½ miles from Ashbourne on the road to Wirksworth, recently much altered as a result of the Carsington Reservoir. Its grey stone houses encircle a

93

Ladybower Dam

small church that is partly Norman and has a thirteenth century font. The Hall is now the post office.

LADYBOWER AND THE DERWENT VALLEY *Map C.4*

WITH THE building of the Ladybower Reservoir, adjacent to Howden Reservoir, the villages of Derwent and Ashopton were completely submerged. The packhorse bridge which once linked Derwent and Hope Woodlands was re-erected at Slippery Stones in memory of the late John Derry, editor of the 'Sheffield Independent' and a writer on Derbyshire. Hursthead Cote (1,280 ft), Crook Hill, Ouzelden Clough, are all on the western side of the Derwent Reservoir and can be reached by footpaths from the Glossop-Sheffield road. Back Tor (1,765 ft), Dovestone Tor (1,656 ft), and White Tor (1,599 ft), are the highest points of Derwent Edge and a track from the Glossop-Sheffield road runs along the ridge. These dams were used by Dr. Barnes Wallis and his team to test his bouncing bomb and the film 'The Dam Busters' telling this interesting story was shot here. Near Derwent Reservoir is a monument to 'Tip' a sheepdog bitch who for 15 weeks guarded the dead body of her master who died in a blizzard.

LANGLEY MILL *Map J.8*

NOT THE prettiest place in Derbyshire. For its size, this 'village' between Heanor and Eastwood has been described as the most highly industrialised area by far in the county. Even in the 1900s it had the Vulcan Iron Works making castings for export all over the world, not to mention factories producing bricks and stone bottles.

Today several important commercial enterprises have their premises here, notably Aristoc Kayser Wolsey, a subsidiary of Courtaulds Hosiery Ltd.; Smith and Sons Flour Mills and Langley Pottery. It draws much of its workforce from its larger neighbour Heanor.

LATHKILL DALE *Map F.4*

BETWEEN MONYASH and Alport the course of the River Lathkill (or Lathkil) forms a beautiful valley in places liberally wooded, while the rock scenery at the upper end is very fine. Here the old river bed is dry, but where Cales Dale comes in from the south the river rises by springs through the limestone floor. Above Over Haddon the water vanishes from time to time, but below the ford at this village it surges up from the bed and flows on to Alport. The valley can be explored on foot, the going being fairly easy. Areas of the Dale form part of the Derbyshire Dales Nature Reserve under the control of the Nature Conservancy Council.

LEA — See under Dethick.

LINTON *Map O.6*

A MODERN parish, now mainly agricultural since the closing of the Coton Park colliery. The church which is of early English style was erected in 1881.

LITTLE EATON *Map K.7*

A GROWING village near Derby on the Alfreton road, with stretches of moor and woodland, and attractive views over the Derwent Vale. Close by is Drum Hill, where the Derby Boy Scouts have a permanent campsite. Severn-Trent Water Limited has a water

Conksbury Bridge in Lathkill Dale

filtration plant and service reservoirs on the high ground to the east of the village. There are many old quarries in the neighbourhood, from one of which came the stone to build the Birmingham Town Hall. 'The Queen's Head' is a fine 18th century inn. From this village came T.P.C. Wilson (son of the local vicar), a forgotten Great War poet and writer, cut off in his prime in the trenches.

LITTLE HUCKLOW *Map D.4*

A HAMLET on the hills above Tideswell, surrounded by old shafts, gravel hillocks and rakes which give evidence of great activity in lead mining a hundred or more years ago. With no church, no shops, this is a place of real seclusion in a bracing countryside.

LITTLE LONGSTONE *Map E.4*

A TYPICAL Derbyshire village situated about three miles from Bakewell, with village stocks in a good state of preservation. A few minutes' walk from the village are Monsal Head and Monsal Dale. The Head provides one of the best viewpoints of the county – of the dale below, with the River Wye running through richly wooded slopes and limestone rocks. Footpaths through the woods and by the river lead downstream to Ashford, or upstream to Cressbrook and Litton Mill via Water-cum-Jolly Dale. The latter path is *not* a public right of way but a concession path.

The Longsdons of Little Longstone Manor have been in occupation for seven centuries.

LITTLEOVER *Map L.6*

See under Derby.

LITTON *Map E.4*

ITS HOUSES grouped around a central square, this village stands in Litton Dale, a mile east of Tideswell. There is an old stone cross and a number of interesting eighteenth century houses. This was the home of William Bagshawe, the seventeenth century preacher, and from this village originated the celebrated family of Lytton of Knebworth.

LOCKO PARK *Map L.8*

'DULCE EST DECIPERE IN LOCO' proclaims lettered ballustrading on one of Derbyshire's lesser known great houses. It is an apposite quote from Horace (Odes 4.XII) as well as being a gentle pun and roughly

95

Locko Park, the seat of the Drury-Lowe family not far from Derby

translated into modern idiom means that it is good to unwind 'at the appropriate time', or perhaps 'in this place'.

Locko is the home of Captain Drury-Lowe and is *not* open to the public but each August the Park forms the venue of the Novice and Intermediate Horse Trial Championships of Great Britain.

The private chapel dates from 1669. The bulk of the house is 17th century by Smith of Warwick. There were additions in 1804 and the biggest ones in 1856 when the tower, picture gallery, big dining room and entrance were added, the architect being H. I. Stevens. In 1896 further west and east wings were added. The 1856 parts were added by William Drury-Lowe, a great Victorian traveller, collector and dilettante. They very much show the Italian influence as a result of his travels there and his love for that country.

LONG EATON Map L.9

LONG EATON lies on the River Trent close to the M1 and has an interesting history. Until the year 603 it was held by the Welsh, and by the Danes until 874. At the time the Domesday Book was compiled, it was known by the Anglo-Saxon name of 'Aitone', meaning 'the town by the water'. After the lapse of several centuries, quarrying activities at Redhill brought fresh stimulus to the district, and early in the nineteenth century, with the construction of turnpike roads, followed by the railways, canals and lace mills, Long Eaton sprang vividly to life. The lace industry on which its prosperity was built is still flourishing, as are a variety of other newer industries.

The Parish Church of St. Laurence was at one time a chapel of ease of Sawley. In 1868 the old chapel – which may well have been erected on the site of a Saxon building – was incorporated in a new church to form the south aisle. There are ample evidences of its Norman origin. The south doorway contains three orders of moulding – double-billet, circular-chain

and beak-head. The semi-circular plain archway between the old nave and chancel is probably earlier, and the same may be said of the deeply-splayed window of the old nave. This is finished with long-and-short work, usually regarded as pre-Norman technique. The chancel has a fourteenth century window with flowing tracery.

The fine stretch of the Trent known as Trent Lock, with facilities for sailing and boating, is within walking distance of the town's centre, and the banks of the Trent and Erewash Canal provide extensive facilities for anglers. The town possesses an enclosed swimming pool which incorporates a sauna bath and solarium, at West Park. Stock car racing, and greyhound racing at the Stadium attract thousands.

On the west side of the town is Trent College, set in 40 acres of grounds and playing fields. The main buildings are over 100 years old and contain a fine chapel. In recent years, there have been many additions to the buildings. Particularly noteworthy are the Kelvin Block, which has been modernised to house the English, Geography and Modern Languages departments, a new Science Block, the Design Area, the Lecture Theatre and Concert Hall. The college, which is a boarding school, also admits dayboys at the age of 11 and girls into the Sixth Form. The school will be wholly co-educational in 1993.

The town possesses a fine Hall by Joseph Pickford (1778) now part of the Council Offices and a Public Library in Tamworth Road, and at the rear is a modern Elder Citizens' Centre set in an attractive garden. At West Park (137 acres) and Sawley Park (8 acres) provision is made for football, hockey, cricket, tennis, bowls and other sports, and Petersham Hall is available for social functions. The town's football club is Long Eaton United and the ground is at Grange Park, which is owned by the Council. There are large free car parks in the centre of the town, at Lawrence Street, Cross Street, Beaconsfield Street and Waverley Street. Long Eaton Railway Station is in Tamworth Road, Sawley. An attractive open-air Market area has been provided between High Street and Tamworth Road. Market days are Friday and Saturday.

LONGFORD Map L.5

THIS RURAL village is situated eight miles from Ashbourne, on the banks of a small stream over which there are two bridges. The Church of St. Chad dates from pre-Norman times, and the tower, along with those of Youlgreave and North Wingfield, is a good example of its kind. Visible from the road is Longford Hall, a late medieval house Georgianised by Pickford in 1762 and restored after a bad fire in 1942. It was the seat of a family of Cokes of Derbyshire for nearly three centuries. Fine monuments to the Cokes and their predecessors the Longfords can be seen in the church. These Cokes descend from Clement Coke, 5th son of Sir Edward Coke, Chief Justice of England. Clement's son, Sir Edward, received a baronetcy which became extinct in 1727. The property passed to descendants of Coke of Norfolk, 1st Earl of Leicester.

LONGNOR (Staffordshire) Map F.3

BOUNDED ON the north by the Dove and on the

south by the Manifold, Longnor stands on the main road from Bakewell to Leek. It is favoured by visitors as a centre for exploring upper Dovedale and the Manifold Valley, while being within easy reach of the amenities of Buxton, which lies some six miles to the north.

The Church of St. Bartholomew is in the Italian style, consisting of nave and an embattled western tower with pinnacles. Its font is of Norman design. In the churchyard can be seen a memorial to a William Billings, who was present at the taking of Gibraltar in 1704, was at the battle of Ramillies in 1706, and also served against the rebellions of 1715 and 1745.

LONG RAKE *Map G.4*

HERE ON the hill top near Arbor Low are many remains of the old open-cast lead workings or rakes – deep vertical cuttings into the limestone where the early miners followed the veins of lead. The surface rakes are usually the very early mines worked many centuries ago. Other open-cast lead workings may have been seen near Castleton and on Masson Hill above Matlock. There are records of lead mining in Derbyshire as far back as Saxon and early Norman times, while pigs of lead have been found stamped with the names of Roman emperors. Lead mining is certainly the oldest industry in the county and is still carried on in certain parts as a by-product.

LONGSHAW *Map D.5*

LONGSHAW LODGE, formerly a shooting box of the Dukes of Rutland, is just south of Sheffield, set in unspoiled moorland. It is now a property of the National Trust and its chief claim to fame is that it is the venue of the annual Longshaw Sheepdog Trials

held here in the first week of September. This event is one of the most important of its kind in the country.

LOSCOE *Map J.8*

MIREY LEYS FARM, in Denby Lane, is of considerable antiquity and has an old Quaker burial ground close by, over the parish boundary. The church is a modern brick structure built in the 1930s, and the pretty farm house dated 1704 by the main cross-roads was once the home of the eminent clock-maker James Woolley.

LOSE HILL *Map C.4*

LOSE HILL (1,563 ft) affords wonderful views of the Hope Valley and Vale of Edale. From Edale the path from Barber Booth is joined. This leads on to Rushup Edge (1,609 ft) and then to Mam Tor (1,700 ft). On Rushup Edge is 'Lord's Seat', a tumulus owned by the National Trust. The 19th century Hall is now a Peak Park residential and educational centre.

LULLINGTON *Map P.5*

LULLINGTON IS a remote and totally peaceful village on the southern border of the county, essentially agricultural. The church has fine stained glass in the chancel windows and the clock was reputedly made by the village blacksmith many years ago. There is a pretty Victorian village hall with carved arms of the Colvile family, former squires, whose seat is near by.

MACKWORTH *Map L.6* see under Derby.

MAM TOR *Map C.3*

THIS BOLD mountain of over 1,700 feet is situated at the western extremity of the beautiful Hope Valley. Near the top is a prehistoric camp some 1,200 yards in

Mam Tor 'The Shivering Mountain' seen from Castleton

circumference, enclosed by a double line of entrenchments. Constantly recurring landslides take place owing to the peculiar composition of shale and grit in alternate layers – a characteristic that has continued for many centuries, and noted in Elizabethan times. The main road (A625) has been completely blocked for some years as the result of a landslide. Light traffic only can approach Castleton from the west. Heavy traffic, including char-a-bancs must take lengthy diversions. Fine views of the Hope Valley and the Vale of Edale are gained from its summit.

MAPPLETON *Map J.4*

AN OLD brick-built village, sometimes called Mapleton, on the Dove near Ashbourne. The little 18th century stone church has a pillared porch surmounted by a dome, and possesses fragments of old glass. A one-arch bridge spans the Dove to carry the road to Okeover Hall, an early 18th century mansion of brick and stone with a distinguished 20th century wing by Marshall Sisson, set in an extensive

The unusual 18th century church at Mappleton

deer park. The Okeovers have owned the estate for many centuries but the Hall had not been used as a residence for a number of years until the late Sir Ian Walker-Okeover had it restored. The village has some interesting almshouses dated 1727, a manor house and nearby is Callow Hall (1852), a neo-Elizabethan house with a tower by Stevens, now an hotel.

MARSTON MONTGOMERY *Map L.3*

CLOSE TO the river Dove and the county boundary, Marston is a quiet village of great age. St. Giles, the parish church, has 10th or 11th century architecture in its chancel arch, a pointed bell tower, and a number of ancient yews around it. The village takes its name from the Montgomery family, to distinguish it from Marston-on-Dove near by. At the cross-roads is the fine timbered Old Hall.

MARSTON ON DOVE *Map M.5*

ONE OF a group of pretty villages on the river Dove between Sudbury and Egginton. The tower of St. Mary's Church houses one of the oldest bells in the

county, cast by John of Stafford in 1366. Hilton, beyond the village on the Derby-Tutbury road was once part of Elizabethan Marston.

St. Giles Church at Marston Montgomery with its pyramidal bellcote, a rare feature in Derbyshire churches

Opposite: High Tor, Matlock, seen from Artists' Corner

MATLOCK *Map G.6*

MATLOCK STANDS on the A6 roughly equidistant from Derby and Buxton. From here roads lead also to Alfreton and Chesterfield and ultimately to the M1 Motorway. This busy town is a centre for exploring the beautiful countryside around, for it is situated at the southern edge of the Peak National Park. A branch line from Derby provides a link with the main railway network. Peak Rail, based at Matlock Station, aims to open a steam service to Buxton.

Matlock was once noted for its many imposing 'Hydros', but today these 'temples of healing by the use of water' are all past history. The buildings, however, remain, being used for a variety of purposes: the largest, 'Smedley's', is now the County Offices; the most ornate, 'Rockside', is now part of the College of Education. Brooding over Matlock is the gloomy, haunted-looking building known as Riber Castle which was built, in the mid 19th century, for his residence, by John Smedley (a textile manufacturer at Lea and the founder of Smedley's Hydro) entirely to his own design, with stone obtained from a local quarry. It is seen to best advantage from the Hall Leys Garden in Matlock, with its gaunt embattled façade frowning on the town from a height of 800 feet. Unoccupied for many years, the Castle, with the surrounding land, was acquired by a group of zoologists who developed the site as a Nature Reserve for British and European Fauna. Riber Hill can be climbed by one or other of the several attractive footpaths.

Due south one passes through a great natural gorge to Matlock Bath (see p. 100). High Tor a massive limestone cliff towers 389 feet above Matlock Dale and the River Derwent. Opposite High Tor, separated only by the gorge, is the 1,100 foot limestone mass of

Masson Hill, the southern tip of which, known as the Heights of Abraham – an association with the death of General Wolfe at Quebec in 1759 – descends sharply into Matlock Bath through a forest of trees. The woodland paths through these trees provide some striking views of Matlock Bath and the surrounding countryside but access is now possible by cable car (see p. 6). The Masson and Rutland Caverns, once worked by the Romans for lead, are approached by way of the Heights and are open to public view, whilst the Victoria Prospect Tower, on the brow of the hill, is not only a prominent landmark but commands extensive and breathtaking views in all directions.

MATLOCK BATH *Map G.6*

ENTERING MATLOCK BATH from the south is an exciting experience. The river Derwent flows close by on the right while on the left and ahead rise steep hills dotted around with early 19th century villas in different architectural styles. These were houses of the well-to-do who came here to 'take the waters', for this was once a well-known spa, though all the once popular establishments are now hardly a memory. Matlock Bath is more dramatic than Malvern and has

Late summer flowers in Hall Leys Gardens, Matlock. Opposite: View of Matlock Bath from the south

The celebrated Victorian Pavilion at Matlock Bath. The boats can be hired

been compared with Switzerland. It has been praised by Byron, Ruskin and other celebrities. A popular resort for generations, today few places of similar size have so much to offer.

Some years ago the road and river in the centre of Matlock Bath were separated by a row of old buildings, but road improvements (which earned a Civic Award) have opened up the river front, and there is now an attractive riverside walk along the whole length of the South and North Parades.

At the time of writing the famous 'Petrifying Well' is closed to the public and its future uncertain but there is a good aquarium.

On the opposite side of the river are the luxuriant Lovers' Walks: a riverside walk flanked by winding hillside paths climbing up the limestone cliffs, far above the river, from which wonderful views can be seen of the quaint town built on the steep slopes of Masson Hill. The Lovers' Walks can be reached either by crossing over the Jubilee Bridge or by using the handsome bridge in the Derwent Gardens.

The Derwent Gardens are the focal point of the annual Illuminations, which from August to October provide a special and popular attraction, particularly when, at weekends, on 'Venetian Nights', the illuminated boats parade up and down the river.

The Peak District Mining Museum, housed in the Pavilion alongside the Tourist Information Office, has exhibits and displays illustrating 2,000 years of lead mining in the Peak. The future location of this impressive and important Museum is, at the time of writing, uncertain, as is the Pavilion itself.

Gulliver's Kingdom is a very popular attraction with many exciting experiences for children (see p. 6). Gulliver's Kingdom is off Temple Road, across the A6 from the Pavilion.

Also on Temple Road, Matlock Bath Model Railway Museum and Exhibition presents model landscape vistas including railway lines of bygone days, with working trains of period design operating on an elaborate automatic system. The landscapes are complete to the smallest detail.

To most visitors the major attraction of the Matlocks is the beauty of the hills and dales; there are many glorious views to be found – from the Black Rocks, from the Wishing Stone, from Farley Lane, from Darley Hillside, from Salters Lane – all these and many others have their devotees. And beyond the district boundaries, but within easy reach, are many famous and historic houses, prehistoric remains and places of ancient custom, and above all, the countryside which became the first of the National Parks.

Sporting facilities are available at Hall Leys Park for tennis etc. and there is a Lido in Matlock. The Tourist Office in the Pavilion is a useful source of information (telephone 0629 55082).

MAYFIELD *Map J.4*

THE HANGING BRIDGE, which is so named because

of the hangings which took place of Scottish rebels during the 1745 rising, crosses the River Dove and joins Derbyshire to Staffordshire. Just over the bridge in Staffordshire is the village of Mayfield, noted for its association with Thomas Moore, who lived in Moore's Cottage at Upper Mayfield. Olivia, Thomas Moore's daughter, who died in early infancy, lies buried in the churchyard. The church of St. John the Baptist dates back to the 12th century but has a notable 14th century chancel and the tower bears the date of 1515. There are two Halls in the village, Old Hall at Middle Mayfield and Mayfield Hall, which is an impressive late Georgian house by Thomas Gardiner of Uttoxeter.

MELANDRA CASTLE *Map B.2*

THIS ROMAN station, at Glossop, measures 120 yards by 112 yards. They called it Ardotalia. Excavations by the Derbyshire Archaeological Society have resulted in some interesting finds, the chief of which are the foundations of the guard chambers and towers.

MELBOURNE *Map N.7*

SET IN pleasant rolling country just south of the Trent, Melbourne has several small industries, but the greater part of the parish is still agricultural land, much of it cultivated by market gardeners. It is eight miles from Derby, and has a reasonable 'bus service.

The place has a long and notable history. It was recorded in Domesday Book as a royal manor. A castle was built here, licence to crenellate an existing house was granted in 1311 to Robert de Hold, and John, Duke of Bourbon, the most important French prisoner taken at Agincourt, was detained here for nineteen years. Mary Queen of Scots, too, was to have been imprisoned at Melbourne, but the castle was found to be too ruinous. It was allowed to fall completely into ruins in the seventeenth century, and only the scantiest remains are left.

St. Michael's Church was built in the late eleventh or early twelfth century. It is a fine example of Norman architecture, with the grandeur of massive simplicity. When it was built it was the largest and most important church in South Derbyshire. The Australian flag hangs inside the church, presented by the Archbishop of Melbourne in 1948. Numerous hatchments of former owners of the Hall have been restored in recent years.

Melbourne Pool and the water-mill recalls the fact that the name Melbourne signifies 'mill stream'. Melbourne Hall is the home of Lord and Lady Ralph Kerr (see p. 21).

In 1837 a tiny settlement in Australia was named after Lord Melbourne. That settlement is now a great city, the capital of Victoria, and relations between the new Melbourne and the old are most cordial.

Thomas Cook, founder of the world-wide travel

Melbourne Pool and Church

agency and benefactor to his native place, was born in Melbourne in 1808.

MELBOURNE HALL *Map N.7* See page 21.

MERMAID'S POOL *Map C.3*
FROM THE heights of Kinder, which stretch away north from Edale Cross, the slopes of this magnificent expanse of mountain land drop 1,000 feet in half a mile. The little Mermaid's Pool lies on the hillside as you look over towards Kinder Downfall. The pool is said to be frequented by a mermaid, a glimpse of whom will confer immortality!

MEYNELL LANGLEY *Map K.6*
THERE HAVE been Meynells at Meynell Langley since the reign of Henry I and though the estate passed to other hands three times in the course of history, the family always came back and are still ensconced in their charming, very English country house set in its magnificent park. House and setting can be glimpsed briefly from the Derby-Ashbourne road.

The family has produced Godfrey, a distinguished antiquarian, Hugo founder of the Meynell Hunt known as 'the Father of English Foxhunting' (he was of another branch at Hoar Cross Hall) and numerous soldiers from a Meynell who fought at Crecy to the late Captain Godfrey Meynell, V.C. Meynell Langley is a private residence and is not open to the public.

MICKLEOVER *Map L.6* See under Derby.

MIDDLETON-BY-WIRKSWORTH
Map H.6
A VILLAGE with some very extensive quarries and

spectacular rock and cliff faces, overlooking the Via Gellia and surrounded by fine and bracing moorland. D. H. Lawrence, the author, who was born on the Derbyshire-Nottinghamshire border at Eastwood, lived for a time at Mountain Cottage, Middleton.

Middleton Top engine house has been restored to working order and can be viewed on certain days.

MIDDLETON-BY-YOULGREAVE
Map G.4
A VERY pretty village in deepest Derbyshire. The celebrated Derbyshire archaeologist, Thomas Bateman, lived at Lomberdale Hall just outside the village and his tomb can be seen nearby topped by a representation of a Bronze Age urn.

Middleton Hall, a fine house belonging to the Waterhouse family, stands in its own park. The old home of the Fulwoods, once squires here, is no longer. Christopher Fulwood, a gallant Cavalier, was shot by Parliamentarians.

MILFORD *Map K.7*
JEDEDIAH STRUTT founded a cotton mill here in 1780 but the date of the present building is not known. The Holy Trinity Church by Moffat, 1848, and the Stone Bridge of 1790, with its two elegant segmental arches, are both interesting pieces of architecture. Milford House, now an old people's home, was designed by William Strutt, FRS, for his father Jedediah, in 1780.

MILLERS DALE and MONSAL DALE
Map E.3, 4
THIS DELECTABLE section of Derbyshire has few

Millers Dale

Monsal Dale and its beautiful viaduct

rivals. The course of the River Wye, a comparatively small stream which joins the Derwent at Rowsley, is only a few miles in length, but it is exceptionally beautiful. Between Bakewell and Rowsley, along the course of the Wye, an especially beautiful stretch has been called 'The Garden of the Peak', and is a valley, with rising hills well wooded, which leads to the junction with the waters of the Bradford and Lathkill. This is a fine section for the angler, famous for trout and grayling. Following the Wye upstream, the visitor passes Haddon to Bakewell, thence to Ashford and Monsal Dale, where the vista becomes glorious as the river rounds the foot of Fin Cop. The railway viaduct at Monsal Dale, which excited the wrath of Ruskin, does not in fact unduly mar the countryside.

From Monsal Dale one passes to Cressbrook Dale, Bull Tor and Eagle Tor, and on to Millers Dale, at which point the whole character of the river changes from a still, peaceful stream to a raging torrent that tumbles, twists and bubbles across the stones about Chee Tor and Chee Dale. It is here that the magnificent rocks, rising to some three hundred feet, overhang the river and dale. And so it is all the way to Ashford Dale, past Lovers' Leap, and to Buxton.

Ruskin, however, in his famous *Fors Clavigera,* wrote of the spoliation of this beautiful Dale: 'That valley where you might expect to catch sight of Pan, Apollo, and the Muses, is now desecrated in order that a Buxton fool may be able to find himself in Bakewell at the end of twelve minutes, and vice versa'.

Ravenstor, a fine modern house and 64 acres of delightful limestone upland and dale, including one mile of the River Wye and Tideswell Gorge, were presented to the National Trust in 1937-38 by Alderman J. G. Graves, of Sheffield, and are leased to the Youth Hostels Association.

MONYASH *Map F.4*

THIS ANCIENT village, situated in wild limestone country, at the upper end of Lathkill Dale, was formerly the lead-mining centre of the High Peak. It became a market town in 1340, and still possesses remains of a market cross of that date. St. Leonard's Church was originally a chapelry of Bakewell, and an early Norman foundation, but the present structure dates principally from the fourteenth century, with the exception of the beautiful triple sedilia and piscina of the Transitional-Norman period. There is a very ancient chest more than seven feet long. At One Ash, in this parish, the monks of Roche Abbey had a grange, and here in later times was the favourite summer resort of John Bright, the famous Radical Quaker statesman and orator of the nineteenth century. Monyash was at one time a Quaker centre.

MORLEY *Map K.8*

THIS VILLAGE has a church (St. Matthew's), dating from Norman times and second to none in Derbyshire in points of interest. It has Norman arcades, fourteenth century south port, chancel and north chapel, a tower and spire of about 1400, and a fifteenth century south chapel; and many monuments and brasses from the fifteenth to the eighteenth centuries, mainly to the Statham and Sacheverell families. The glory of the church, however, is the magnificent medieval stained glass, brought from Dale Abbey and now in the fine north chapel.

Broomfield Hall, on the Derby road, is the Derbyshire County Council's residential Farm Institute, while Morley Manor by the great Victorian architect G. F. Bodley is a Dr. Barnado's home. The parish contains part of the Roman Ryknield Street.

MORTON *Map G.8*

ALTHOUGH MENTIONED in Domesday, much of the old Church of The Holy Cross, Morton, was rebuilt in 1850, but the Tower, dated about 1400, contains Norman gargoyles and several stones which appear part of a Saxon tomb. The North Arcade of circular piers is typical thirteenth-century work.

The Church has a plain Saxon font, Jacobean pulpit and altar, while the chancel screen of great beauty, contains tracery of the 1400 period, stated to have formed part of the Foljambe screen in Chesterfield Parish Church. Some 19 'initial and date' stones in the churchyard, period 1673 to 1734, are worthy of note, whilst a record exists of the names of Rectors of Morton from 1252 to the present date.

MUGGINTON and MERCASTON
Map K.6

SEVEN MILES from Derby, Mugginton Church (All Saints') dates from the twelfth century and the register from 1764. The Intake Chapel, some distance from the church, is a very small building overshadowed by yew trees. The amusing story of its origin concerns a man named Francis Brown who lived about the beginning of the eighteenth century. In a drunken state of mind, and against his wife's wishes, he decided to ride to Derby one black night. Having secured his horse, he discovered to his chagrin that the animal had horns and he concluded it must be the Devil. The shock made him senseless. On recovering, so great was his alarm that he became a sobered man and built a chapel in 1723, which he endowed at his death – the present Intake Chapel. He had, of course, haltered a cow in his fuddled state.

NETHER PADLEY *Map D.5*

WITH FROGGATT Edge and Burbage Moor short distances away, Nether Padley, on the banks of the Derwent near Grindleford Bridge, is situated amongst some of the most splendid scenery in Derbyshire. The church is not very old but stands on an earlier site.

NETHERSEAL *Map P.6*

A PICTURESQUE village on the southern borders of the county (part of Leicestershire until 1897). St. Peter's Church, mainly of the nineteenth century, contains a fifteenth century tomb, with the effigy of a priest in full canonicals, representing a former rector. Three miles away on 'No Man's Heath' is a very old stone of four sides, probably indicating ancient boundary lines of Derby, Leicester, Warwick and Staffordshire. Near Dead Dane Bottom is a burial barrow. The Tudor Hall has been demolished but the charming Old Hall remains.

NEWHAVEN *Map G.4*

AN ANCIENT coaching inn hotel on the main Ashbourne-Buxton road, at the junction of roads to Matlock and Bakewell, well situated for exploring the Low Peak.

NEW MILLS *Map C.1*

THE INDUSTRIAL town derives its name from corn mills on the Kinder streams. It has behind it a tradition, dating from the Industrial Revolution, of association with the Lancashire cotton industry, which found in New Mills the special conditions necessary for its operations, and from the end of the eighteenth century the district has enjoyed a large measure of prosperity. Large parts of the district are still rural in character and devoted to agriculture. There is also some very fine hill country within the district and the hamlet of Rowarth in the northern part is popular with tourists and climbers – the heights of Kinder being within easy reach. The Peak District National Park includes much of these parts. High Lea Hall estate, with fourteen acres of delightfully wooded land, has been acquired by the Council as a public park. The nine-hole course of the New Mills Golf Club at Shaw Marsh enjoys a large membership and welcomes visitors. A swimming pool and squash courts are among facilities in the town.

NEWTON SOLNEY *Map N.6*

THREE MILES from Repton, Newton Solney church, of Norman origin, contains beautiful monuments of the de Solneys, who held the manor in the thirteenth century. One of these monuments surmounts an altar tomb in the form of an alabaster recumbent knight in armour and is in a fair state of preservation. Several restorations of the building have taken place, but some portions of the original chancel arch and a doorway in the north aisle show Norman traces. Within the parish is Bladon Castle an extraordinary building, part house and part folly. Designed to look immense on the skyline it is, in fact, a modest dwelling. It was once called 'Hoskin's Folly' after its builder. Its skyline is like a miniature Windsor Castle, which is not surprising as it was probably designed by George IV's architect Sir Jeffry Wyatville. The mansion of Newton Park has been converted into an hotel. It was the earliest Italianate house to be built in

Bladon Castle or Hoskin's Folly at Newton Solney

Derbyshire and was designed by J. Bernasconi in 1798.

NORBURY *Map K.3*

THIS VILLAGE on the River Dove occupies a beautiful position and is a favourite haunt of discriminating anglers. The fishing is, of course, preserved. Situated on an eminence overlooking the river, Norbury Church is probably one of the most

Norbury Church

beautiful village churches to be found in England. As spacious as the nave, the chancel contains much fine architectural detail and many monuments, while an unusually large amount of stained glass of the fourteenth and fifteenth centuries survives. The chancel was erected by Henry Kniveton, rector from 1349 to 1395, and has saw-teeth parapets and large buttresses. The register dates from 1686, and the graveyard is notable for its venerable yew.

The gazebo at the Old Manor House, Norbury, built single-handed by Mr. Rory Young in the late 1970s

Nearby is the Fitzherberts' fine fifteenth century house, Norbury Manor, which was enlarged in the reign of Queen Anne. It contains much fine panelling and some rare stained glass. Behind is one of the earliest surviving examples of domestic architecture in England, the remains of the first Fitzherbert house built in 1250 and now restored to its former state. The property was bought by the late Mr. Marcus Stapleton-Martin who restored it and left it in his will to the National Trust. It is now occupied by tenants who are Fitzherbert descendants and not open to the public.

NORTH WINGFIELD *Map F.8*

ON THE road from Clay Cross to Heath, North Wingfield is about five miles south-east of Chesterfield. The fifteenth century Blue Bell Inn was once the Chantry House, where Sir John Babington established a chantry in 1488. St. Lawrence's Church has a bell over 300 years old, and a Norman east doorway in the north aisle is made to look like a window.

OCKBROOK *Map L.8*

OCKBROOK IS situated between Derby and Nottingham and covers an area of 2,122 acres. The church of All Saints has a west tower of the 13th century. The font is Norman and has interlaced arches. The chancel screen came from Wyggeston

Hospital, Leicester, and is generally considered to be 15th century work.

The Moravian Settlement was founded in 1750. The chapel of 1751-2 has adjoining brick-built houses. As Ockbrook School it is a flourishing academy for girls.

OLD BRAMPTON *Map E.7*
ON THE old road from Chesterfield to Baslow, this village well merits a visit. The Church of SS Peter and Paul is of Norman origins. Battlemented walls, a short octagonal spire set on a square base and *c.*1300 sculptures let into the south aisle walls make the church one of great interest.

Over the road from the church is Brampton Hall, a twelfth century building of immense historical interest with fine plaster ceilings and cruck oak beams and oak timbers reputed to have come from an earlier village church. Early records show a passage from one of the cellars to the altar in Old Brampton church on the north side and to an outlet on the south side of the Hall. The Dixon family lived at the Hall for 112 years.

OLD WHITTINGTON *Map E.7*
See under Whittington.

OSMASTON *Map K.4*
THIS PICTURESQUE model estate is 2½ miles from Ashbourne. Osmaston Manor is approached from the village by a lime avenue. Completed about 1865 and a fine example of the architecture of the period, the manor had a magnificent setting in a well-timbered park overlooking several lakes. It was built for the Wright family, ironmasters, and later came into possession of the Walker family. It was demolished

Thatched cruck cottage at Osmaston

by Sir Ian Walker-Okeover in 1966. The annual show of the Ashbourne Shire Horse Society is held in the park in August. The register of the Church of St. Martin in the village dates from 1606 though the present building is Victorian and designed by H. I. Stevens.

OVER HADDON *Map F.4, 5*
A HAMLET on a rocky eminence overlooking the lovely Lathkill Dale. A perfect village centre for walking or angling, with good accommodation, two miles from Bakewell. The village possess a beautifully situated modern church.

OVERSEAL *Map O.6*
COVERING MORE than 2,000 acres, Overseal has important stoneware and pipe works. The church of St. Matthew was consecrated in 1841.

PARLSEY HAY *Map G.4*
ONCE A station on the Cromford and High Peak Railway, which was, at 1,163 feet, one of the highest railway points in England. It is now the junction of the High Peak and Tissington Trails which are popular with walkers, cyclists and horse riders alike.

PARWICH *Map H.4*
NEAR ANCIENT earthworks in which many antiquities have been found. In 1873 St. Peter's Church replaced an ancient structure said to be over 800 years old. From this church are preserved a Norman doorway and chancel arch and a carved tympanum. A prominent feature of the village is the fine brick hall of 1741, formerly seat of the Crompton-Inglefields and now the home of the Shields family.

Sheep-shearing at Parwich

PEAK DALE *Map D.3*
THIS VILLAGE lies south-east of Chapel-en-le-Frith between Buxton and Tideswell. Batham Gate, the Roman track from Brough to Buxton, passes through Peak Dale.

PEAK FOREST *Map D.3*
FIVE MILES from Buxton, and four from Chapel-en-le-Frith, the small village of Peak Forest may be described as the 'Gretna Green' of Derbyshire. In the past many romantic marriages took place after a long chase over the moorlands. To such an extent had this runaway marriage developed in 1725 that steps were taken to check its growth, and this was done by the Fleet Street Marriage Act of 1753. The irregularities in connection with these marriages were enhanced by the fact that the minister was his own surrogate, granted marriage licences, proved wills, and held a

The Church of King Charles the Martyr at Peak Forest

seal of office, being entitled to the following designation: 'Principal Official and Judge in Spiritualities in the Peculiar Court of Peak Forest'. The old church, which was erected in 1657, has been removed. The present Church of King Charles the Martyr built by the 7th Duke of Devonshire in 1877 contains one bell dated 1657, and registers dating from 1669. Christian, Countess of Devonshire, built the original church. Her remarkable devotion to the Royalist cause, however, caused her second and favourite son, Charles Cavendish, to lose his life at the hands of the Parliamentarians in 1643.

PENTRICH *Map H.7*
THE CENTRE of the 'revolution of 1817' which was never dangerous and was firmly crushed. St. Matthew's Church dates from Norman times, and has been frequently restored. It is approached by a long flight of steps. A stone pedestal sundial in the village dates from 1660.

PILSLEY *Map G.8*
A PLEASANT hill-top village, which was, until the pits were sunk, just a hamlet at the southern tip of the parish of North Wingfield. It is mentioned in the Domesday Book. With the sinking of the mines it grew and is now a separate parish with modern housing, although there still remain a few of the stone cottages. The Parish Church, built in 1873, is dedicated to St. Mary the Virgin and has some fine stained glass. Since the closing of the colliery and the railway, the land has been reclaimed and a European award for this scheme was made to the County Council by the Ministry.

PILSLEY *Map E.5*
PART OF the Chatsworth estate this small village has some very attractive stone houses and magnificent views. The school was built in 1849 to the design of Joseph Paxton. It is not be confused with the larger place 6 miles S.E. of Chesterfield.

PINXTON *Map H.9*
FORMERLY A mining village its industrialism is now more widely based. It has early associations with the Industrial Revolution – coal mining and pottery as well as being on a branch of the Erewash Canal and a

terminus of the early Pinxton-Mansfield tramway. John King, a local man, invented a mine cage safety-detaching hook still in use. An old tradition associates Pinxton with 'Fair Rosamund' Clifford, the mistress of King Henry II.

Roger Sacheverell Coke, of Brookhill Hall, the composer, in his Music Room in Brookhill Stables, seated at his Steinway (now in Alfreton Hall)

The M1 motorway passes very close to Pinxton and tears through Brookhill Park the former seat of the Cokes of Brookhill. It was this family which started the pottery producing the now famous and rare Pinxton China. The last male of the family was the composer Roger Sacheverell Coke who lived at the Hall until his death in 1972. He composed very much in the romantic style and was much influenced by Rachmaninov who was a personal friend. The Hall has been sold and restored but much of the estate has passed through the female line to the Darwins.

PLEASLEY *Map F.9*
THIS PRETTY village is situated on a ridge to the east of the River Meden. Its church dates back to the 13th century and the registers from 1553. There are remains of a medieval village cross.

POOLE'S CAVERN *Map E.2*
POOLE'S HOLE or Cavern, below Grin Low, Buxton, is an enormous cave famous for its stalactite and stalagmite formations, and is open to visitors. It derives its name from an outlawed member of the Pole family of Hartington Hall back in the 15th century.

QUARNDON *Map K.7*
DESPITE CONSIDERABLE development, this is still a place of quiet byways, with a pleasant village street. There are extensive views of Kedleston Park, Duffield, Allestree Park and the Derwent's Vale. It once had a spa and the well-head, its only survival, can be seen in the village.

RADBOURNE *Map L.6*

ON A QUIET secondary road off the main Ashbourne-Derby road lies this unspoilt village. In a rich agricultural district, it is yet only a few miles from the centre of Derby. Radburne *(sic)* Hall, built between 1742 and 1744 by William Smith of Warwick, is a good example of Georgian architecture. St. Andrew's Church contains some interesting monuments to the Pole family. The house is *not* open to the public.

RENISHAW *Map D.9*

A LARGISH industrial village between the M1 and Sheffield. Its industry long pre-dates the Industrial Revolution as an ironworks was founded by the Sitwell family in about 1640 so that before 1700 the Sitwells were the world's biggest manufacturers of nails. The ironworks was sold in 1792 but it continued to flourish. The area also had a long association with coalmining.

The Sitwell Arms, one of the village's few distinguished buildings, underwent radical changes some years ago to convert it from a country pub to a modernised hotel with an *haute cuisine* restaurant named after John Piper, the distinguished artist who painted many scenes hereabouts. On the 'golden heights' above the village stands the seat of the Sitwell family, Renishaw Hall.

RENISHAW HALL *Map D.9*

'THOUGH THIS lovely country teems with industry, every prospect is idyllic, and chimneys in the distance become tall obelisks'. So wrote Sir Osbert Sitwell of Renishaw and its surroundings, and indeed the hugger mugger of 19th century industries and

Radburne Hall, the seat of the Chandos-Pole family. The spelling of the house differs from that of the village

Renishaw Hall, from the gardens and right, Sir George and Lady Ida Sitwell with Edith, Sacheverell and Osbert by J. S. Sargent

railways, of pylons and chimneys have settled into a curious harmony with the stone walls and country house parks of the rural landscape with the ever looming presence of Sheffield all too short a distance to the north.

To countless people Renishaw Hall is a familar place even though they have never set eyes upon it, for it has been described in the prose and poetry of Sir Osbert Sitwell, his brother Sir Sacheverell Sitwell and his sister Dame Edith Sitwell. Between them the three Sitwells contributed a large share of great literature and poetry to the 20th century, apart from immortalising their family home.

Over the last hundred years the appearance of Renishaw and its incomparable gardens owes most to Sir George Sitwell and his grandson, the present owner, Sir Reresby Sitwell and his wife Penelope. Sir George redesigned much of the landscape and the present owners have improved upon it apart from planting one of the most northerly vineyards in the world and actually producing wine from it.

The gardens are open to the public on certain days of the year as advertised in the press.

The Hall was built about 1625 and greatly enlarged in the late 18th and early 19th centuries by Sir Sitwell Sitwell to the designs of Joseph Badger, a Sheffield architect. The greatest architect of the 20th century, Sir Edwin Lutyens, was also involved in the early 1900s. He remodelled the lobby still known as the Billiard Room that connects the Great Drawing Room with the Ball Room that served as a chapel in the Victorian age, and years later he redesigned part of Renishaw Park Golf Clubhouse for his friend, Sir George.

REPTON *Map N.6*

THIS PLACE, probably the first capital of Mercia, is situated on ground overlooking the River Trent. It was an important religious centre many centuries before the foundation of the Priory in Plantagenet times. The first Christian church of the converted English was probably erected here on the arrival of four priests from Northumbria in the seventh century. Diuma, the leader of this missionary company, was subsequently made Bishop of Mercia. He was the first of those whose labours sanctified Repton and led to the foundation of Lichfield as a child of the earlier centre. His work began at Repton in 653, according to the Venerable Bede, and we may reasonably assume that this was the time of the founding of the Anglian monastery. The monastery was sacked by the Danes in 874-5 and lay in ruins for about two centuries, after which a church was built on the site of which the present east end (c. AD 750-800, rebuilt in the 930s) is the remainder. The monastery was not rebuilt.

Although of small dimensions, the crypt (c. AD 750) of St Wystan's is one of the most important survivals of Saxon architecture in England, the roof being supported by four spiral columns. It was the burial place of Mercian kings.

The Priory was founded under the will of the Countess of Chester about 1172, and was dissolved at

The old Priory gateway at Repton which now serves as the entrance to Repton School, one of Derbyshire's four public schools

the Reformation. On the site of the ruins Repton School was established under the will of Sir John Port of Etwall in 1557.

During the civil war of 1138-1154 the Earl of Chester built a modest castle here incorporating Danish earthworks.

The famous public school with its fine chapel occupies some remains of the old priory. The fourteenth century Priory Gateway is in good preservation, but the Guest Hall, where the school was begun, is the most interesting part.

RIBER *Map G.6*

JOHN SMEDLEY'S towered and castellated mansion looking like Count Dracula's castle was built in 1862 and is a prominent landmark visible for many miles. Long unoccupied, Riber Castle and its grounds were purchased in 1962 by a group of zoologists, who established there a Fauna Reserve and wildlife parks

Riber Castle

with a most interesting collection of British and European birds and animals, including some very rare and endangered species. The grounds are open all the year round, and provide panoramic views of the Derwent Valley. There is also a cafeteria, licensed bar, children's playground, picnic areas and a souvenir shop.

Riber Hall (1662), now an hotel and restaurant, and the Manor House are examples of Elizabethan and seventeenth century architecture.

RIDDINGS *Map H.8*

ON THE eastern border of the county. The seeker of rural beauty or the lover of broad unspoiled landscapes will never make his way to Riddings, says one writer. Yet there are historical matters which are sufficiently provocative to arouse unusual interest in the place. Oil shale was discovered in the area during the earlier part of last century and proved a successful commercial proposition for twenty years in addition to establishing the fortune of a hitherto unknown Scotsman, James Young, who made the world's first paraffin wax candles. Thereafter he was known as 'Paraffin' Young.

RIPLEY *Map J.8*

RIPLEY STANDS high up and whichever way you may approach the town you are faced with a climb. From beside the old village green, now the Market Place, a high vantage point offers views across the valleys of the Rivers Amber and Derwent and distantly into the foothills of Peakland.

The earliest associations of the Ripley area stretch back to the Roman period when Ryknield Street passed nearby, with evidence of a small Roman Station at Coneygrey Farm. Ripley itself was first christened by the Anglo-Saxons, who so called it after an Old English tribal name (Hrype) or because of the

fact that it was settlement clearing in the form of a strip of land. Domesday Book refers to "Ripelie" and "Pentric" Manors.

Much of the Norman and early medieval history of Ripley can be gleaned from the Charters of the Abbey of Darley, during which period, AD 1251 to be precise, Henry III was prevailed upon by the Abbot of Darley to grant a weekly market and annual Fair to the town. Henry III was staying at the Abbey during a hunting session at Duffield Forest. A copy of this Charter is still displayed in the Council buildings.

Padley Hall, in the valley below Ripley is a fine example of a small Elizabethan Manor House, and is now restored and in private ownership.

Ripley featured early and strongly in the Industrial revolution. Situated as it was in the rich iron and coal fields of Derbyshire, this rural area soon developed into a town. Butterley Company, of which Benjamin Outram was a founder, was formed in 1792 to exploit the local mineral wealth. One of the earliest of Colliery railway tracks known as the 'Outram Way' was laid from Ripley to meet the canal at Little Eaton. The Cromford Canal came by in 1793, the Derby to Chesterfield Turnpike road came in 1806, and the Railway in 1856. Suddenly, Ripley emerged not only as an important centre for coal and iron but also as a trading area. Here in 1860 the Ripley Co-operative Society was born and from such small beginnings the town has developed into a shopping complex, attracting visitors from many surrounding rural villages.

The Town Hall commands the Market Place and was originally built in 1880 as a Market Hall. An eccentric building, it is one of Ripley's most attractive and notable features.

The intensive industrial period left many scars in the area, but efforts have been made to cover them and reclaim the land for further development.

Other facilities include the leisure centre on Derby Road, the new Community Centre near Mill Hill Comprehensive School (formerly the Benjamin Outram School) and a modern library in the town centre.

Butterley Hall (17th century), once the centre of the early Industrial development, is now the Headquarters of the Derby and Derbyshire Constabulary, and in the same vicinity of Butterley Works, is the Midland Railway Centre, a Railway Museum with working steam trains along a track of the old industrial line. See page 4.

Ripley twinned with Lons-le-Saunier in 1970 and it has maintained continual contact since then, naming one of its housing developments after its French twin.

RISLEY *Map L.9*

AN ATTRACTIVE village midway between Derby and Nottingham, with some good eighteenth century houses. The Church of All Saints, built in 1593, is a rare Elizabethan church. The scholastic buildings are memorable, particularly the 1706 Latin house, now restored and resplendent and one of the best houses of its period in this part of England. Risley Hall is mainly Victorian with 1975 municipal additions.

ROCESTER *Map L.3*

A STAFFORDSHIRE village set between the Rivers

Dove and Churnett just over the Derbyshire border, and once a Roman station.

The church here was restored in 1873 and has a fine window with ten scenes from Christ's life painted by William de Morgan, the Pre-Raphaelite. The churchyard contains a seven hundred year old inter-laced-work cross shaft, thought to be the best preserved of its kind in England.

J. C. Bamford (Excavators) Ltd, was founded in Rocester in 1949. Its vast premises cover the place where the Rocester Cheese Market factory once was. Richard Arkwright introduced a textile mill here in 1781.

Nearby also is Abbotsholme School founded by Cecil Reddie, forerunner of the outdoor activity style school. Here flourishes the famous Abbotsholme Arts Society founded by the late Gordon Clark.

THE ROOSDYCHE *Map D.1*
THE ROOSDYCHE, Whaley Bridge, is a remarkable indentation in the side of the hill which has been attributed to the Romans but is probably a natural formation; it varies from 10 to 30 feet, is half a mile in length, and 40 yards wide, enclosed by earth banks.

ROSLISTON *Map O.5*
IN THE south of the county, this village lies close to the Staffordshire border. The grey sandstone building of the church of St. Mary the Virgin was almost entirely rebuilt in 1810 but it still possesses a tower and spire of the early fourteenth century.

ROSTON *Map K.3*
THIS VILLAGE is the setting for much of George Eliot's 'Adam Bede', and houses connected with the story are well preserved.

ROWSLEY *Map F.5*
FROM THE Square, with its famous Peacock Hotel, one can strike out northwards up Church Lane to Haddon Woods – across the Wye Bridge and up Peak Tor to Stanton – or across the Derwent and take a bee-line to Fallinge and the grouse moors. The British track up to Peak Tor which connected the early settlements in Stanton with similar habitations

The Peacock Hotel, Rowsley

near Wessington Common – along which in later days saddlemen used to convey lead to Chesterfield – has recently been much improved. Peak Tor itself, with its vallum, is worth careful examination, as also is Chez Knoll, another early Celtic settlement. The most interesting and attractive of the walks from Rowsley is that on the east side of the Derwent to Beeley and then through the lovely park of Chatsworth to the great house itself, a distance of four miles. Caudwell's Mill is an old mill now restored and making animal provender. It can be seen by the public. See page 6.

The church, built in 1855, is of no particular interest, except that the Rutland Chapel contains a very beautiful altar tomb, by Calder Marshall, to Lady John Manners first wife of the 7th Duke of Rutland. In the church is also preserved the head of a ninth century cross found in the River Wye some years ago. The 'Triquetra' symbol, which is to be found on the Hexham frith stool, is carved on the three arms of this cross. These crosses were sometimes boundary marks, or preaching crosses, or market crosses, or commemorative of some Christian event. The Peacock Hotel was built as a private residence by John Stevenson in 1652; hence the inscription over the doorway. This John Stevenson was the 'man of affairs' to Grace, Lady Manners (the mother of the 8th Earl of Rutland), who founded the Bakewell School in 1636. When the Nag's Head and Red Lion – the old posting houses in the Square – were closed down in 1828, the Peacock became an hotel displaying the Rutland crest of a peacock. Well-dressing takes place here in June.

RUSHUP EDGE *Map C.3*
FLANKING THE Chapel — Mam Tor — Hope road this point is above 1,400 feet and rises, near Mam Tor, to 1,700 feet.

SANDIACRE *Map L.9*
THE CHURCH is famous locally for its beautiful fourteenth century chancel, which is remarkably spacious, and a fine example of the architectural skill of the period. It is claimed that this magnificent chancel is the handiwork of Bishop Norbury. The register dates from 1570. The church is pre-Norman in foundation and there are some Norman remains. There are public sporting facilities at the Sports Centre at Friesland School.

SAWLEY *Map M.9*
HERE THERE is a fine old church which is among the earliest in Derbyshire. A band of monks, rowing down the Trent from Repton, built the first church in these riverside meadows, and as early as 822 it was a prebend of Lichfield so wealthy as to be called 'The Golden Prebend' by William of Malmesbury. Much of the present structure is fourteenth century, with tower and spire and other features of the fifteenth century. The chancel arch is Saxon and the magnificent stone screen is 500 years old. Other treasures include a 600-year old font, a fifteenth century oak screen with an embattled cornice, a Jacobean pulpit with a canopy, a seventeenth century altar table, Elizabethan oak benches and much fifteenth century timbering. There is a former turnpike bridge across the River Trent, and nearby is Sawley Lock, a well-

known centre for motor boating enthusiasts. Also nearby is Trent Lock, local beauty spot and venue for sailing and fishing.

SCARCLIFFE *Map F.9*

AN ESSENTIALLY agricultural parish south of Bolsover and near the Nottinghamshire border, the village offers a church in which lies one of Derbyshire's most charming monuments – the alabaster tomb of Constantia de Frecheville and her child. The legend of Lady Constantia, who is said still to wander the woods around Scarcliffe with her small daughter, is perpetuated in the annual ringing of the curfew bells at Christmas. The River Poulter has its source here and the famous springs, which are reputed to give more water in the summer than in the winter, may be seen.

SCROPTON *See under Foston.*

SHARDLOW and GREAT WILNE *Map M.8*

ON THE border of Leicestershire, Shardlow was by way of being a considerable port on the River Trent at the time when river transport was the best means of taking heavy goods from one part of the country to another. The river runs parallel to the main road through Shardlow leading to the M1 access point at Kegworth. It is after leaving the main road and exploring the older parts of Shardlow that one finds its real beauty. It is a favourite rendezvous in the summer months for boating on the canal and the river, and some charming inns make exploration of this village additionally attractive. Shardlow Marina, started in 1975 is very popular.

On the other side of the road from the church is Shardlow Hall, formerly seat of the Sutton family, designed by Smith of Warwick and Joseph Pickford.

SHEFFIELD (YORKS) *Map C.7*

SHEFFIELD, THE fourth city in England, demands a place in the Guide. Many of her inhabitants live in Derbyshire; thousands more find pleasure and relaxation in its hills and dales.

Of all the great industrial cities of England, Sheffield was by far the most attractive and once had a considerable, if murky, charm. German bombs and modern planners have in recent decades ripped it to shreds but it still retains something of its old magic. Once it was described as 'a mucky picture in a golden frame' because of its close proximity to some of England's most beautiful countryside. Now it is no longer smoky and soot-stained and its public buildings have been cleaned up. Like Rome it is built on hills and embraces several charming villages on its boundaries. To the south some of these were formerly in Derbyshire. Dore, for instance, where the unification of England under King Egbert was effected in 827, Totley an attractive residential place and Abbeydale. Here one will find the Abbeydale Industrial Hamlet, a miraculously preserved 18th century industrial complex for making scythes etc. complete with workmen's cottages, water-wheels, a giant tilt-hammer and even such ephemera as crucible pots. Upon such manufactories lay the great fame and reputation of Sheffield as a steel centre.

Sheffield has a cathedral, a university, art galleries and a museum. In the fine Georgian Cutlers' Hall is held the famous annual Cutlers' Feast.

The old Clock Warehouse, now Hoskin's Wharf, and Canal Wharf, Shardlow

Sunset near Sheldon

SHELDON *Map F.4*

THREE MILES from Bakewell, on a hill 1,000 feet above sea level, Sheldon offers many fine view-points. Fantastic rock formations are to be seen near the old Magpie lead mine, half-a-mile from the village, giving rise to much local talk about 'Druids'. Magpie Mine is the finest lead-mining relic in Britain. Visiting parties are organised by the Peak District Mining Museum. Many tracks were formed by lead miners in this district as elsewhere in the lead-mining areas. Although held in union with Ashford, Sheldon Church enjoys all the rights and privileges of a parish church. Strangely, the old church was under the patronage of All Saints, but a new building was consecrated in 1865 in the name of St. Michael and All Angels. Sheldon Church is very beautiful within and deserves to be more widely known than it appears to be. The old school was given to the people of Sheldon by the 10th Duke of Devonshire after the last war and renamed Hartington Hall in memory of his son, the

Marquess of Hartington (brother of the 11th Duke) who was killed in action.

SHIPLEY PARK *Map K.8*

PART RESTORED industrial waste land and part noble private park to Shipley Hall (another casualty in the ranks of Derbyshire's beautiful houses), Shipley Hall Country Park is approached from the Derby-Heanor road through a sprawling, dreary wilderness of an 'industrial estate'. Then follows a great deal of concrete, asphalt, curbstones and other unsightly emanations of the municipal mind before one begins to sense (this on a wet autumn afternoon) John Betjeman's 'mushroomy, pinewoody, evergreen smells'. Then, unfolding itself in the hollow below you is Shipley Park with its lake, aquatic birds, squirrels and other wildlife. There are relics of the old estate such as the Home Farm and the lodges by the distinguished architects Sir Edwin Lutyens and W. E. Nesfield. There is also a pretty little Gothic dairy.

Part of Shipley Park is now 'The American Adventure'. See p. 6.

Shipley was once the seat of the Miller Mundys (one of the Mundy family married the Miller heiress to Shipley and added the name to his own). It was a very pretty classical house built in 1700 with 1788 additions. It contained portraits by Reynolds, Hoppner and others and in the 1900s was visited by Edward VII and General Sir Redvers Buller. The Miller Mundys moved out in 1922 and, after standing derelict for years after mining subsidence had damaged it, the house was pulled down in 1943.

SHIRLAND *Map G.8*

THIS VILLAGE, two miles from Alfreton, is an ancient settlement the history of which is ultimately connected with the famous family of the Greys of East Derbyshire. The Revell family are also commemorated here. The church is chiefly a fifteenth century structure. The monumental recess in the church is probably a memorial of Sir Henry Grey (fourteenth century). There are many effigies, tombs, etc., of the de Greys. In this church there is a chained copy of Jewell's *Apology* (1609). The register dates from 1675.

SHIRLEY *Map K.5*

A PRETTY village containing a fine church and a very old inn. Nearby flows Sutton Brook. From here came Sewallis (d. c.1129) ancestor of the great family of Shirley, Earls Ferrers and of the Shirleys of Ettington. The moated Hall is now a farm but the Shirleys still own land here and Viscount Tamworth, the heir to Earl Ferrers, lives in the former Vicarage.

SHUTTLEWOOD and STANFREE *Map E.9*

LYING NORTH of Bolsover and six miles east of Chesterfield, these two villages are situated in a mining area.

SMALLEY *Map K.8*

A SMALL village near Heanor pleasantly placed on breezy uplands. Stainsby Hall, now demolished and rebuilt in modern style, was for generations the home of the Wilmot-Sitwell family.

SMISBY *Map O.7*

A CHURCH mainly of the thirteenth and fourteenth centuries in grey sandstone, with several interesting monuments, and a village 'Round House', used in former times as a lock-up, are the principal features of this tiny hamlet, two miles from Ashby-de-la-Zouch. In this village the tournament described by Sir Walter Scott in *Ivanhoe* is reputed to have been held. Some old panelling in the church is said to have come from Ashby Castle. The Hall is of early Tudor origin but is now reduced.

SNAKE ROAD *Map B.2-C.6*

WINDING ITS way from Sheffield to Glossop, this road usually becomes impassable at some time in every winter. At all times spectacularly beautiful, it gives magnificent views of the Peakland heights. Snake Inn stands at map square B.3.

The wild and desolate scenery around Snake Pass

SNELSTON *Map K.4*

THE CHURCH is a nineteenth century structure, but the tower remains from an earlier church. The thirteenth century font gives evidence of the antiquity of the foundation, and the register dates from 1572. There is good fishing in this district, which is near to the famous River Dove. Snelston Hall, the high Victorian Gothic seat of the Stantons, has been demolished, and the family now lives in the beautifully converted stable block.

SOLOMON'S TEMPLE *Map E.2*

THIS INTERESTING landmark crowns the hill at Grin Low, the site of a tumulus, at an elevation of 1,445 feet above sea level. From here fine views of the surrounding country are obtained. It is only a short distance from Buxton.

SOMERSAL HERBERT *Map L.3*

THIS OLD village, which is sometimes called Church Somersal, was the ancestral seat of the Fitzherbert

Somersal Hall at Somersal Herbert

117

South Wingfield Manor

family, who occupied Somersal Hall continuously from the thirteenth century until comparatively recently. The Hall is an ancient and picturesque mansion, half-timbered, with gables which are ornamental. In the churchyard there is an early cross, complete with steps and shaft, much restored. The registers date from 1537.

SOUTH NORMANTON *Map H.9*

THE BIRTHPLACE of Jedediah Strutt, South Normanton is in the heart of a busy industrial district, at Junction 28 of the M1. Details of St. Michael's Church date from the 13th century but the building is mainly 19th century. There is some interesting plate, an engraved Norman coffin stone and a Norman font, and a monument to Robert Revel, 1714, who lived at nearby Carnfield Hall, an Elizabethan mansion with twin gables. This house has recently been restored. Remains of a post windmill exist on Normanton Common. Industrial estates have been developed in the Parish.

SOUTH WINGFIELD *Map H.7*

SITUATED CLOSE to the Amber Valley, the parish of South Wingfield has many historic associations and was once an important coaching point in the eighteenth century. It has a thirteenth century church, but its main claim to fame is the magnificent ruin of Wingfield Manor which is at the top of a low hill and can be seen from several angles. The Manor House is closed owing to its deteriorated condition but the Department of the Environment is carrying out extensive works of preservation with a view to the building being open to the public. It was built by Ralph, Lord Cromwell, in the fifteenth century at the time when military considerations were giving place to domestic amenities.

On the west side of the inner court are remains of the apartments in which Mary Queen of Scots was imprisoned in 1569 and 1584-5. The Banqueting Hall and the crypt beneath it are particularly striking examples of domestic work of the fifteenth century. The Manor House was held alternately by Royalists and Parliamentarians during the Civil War. It was eventually taken by the latter and dismantled by the Haltons in 1774 to build the near-by Hall. The Derbyshire County Show (in June) is now held in Wingfield Park between South Wingfield and Ambergate (tel: 0602 324653).

SPINKHILL *Map D.9*

ALMOST A Roman Catholic enclave. Mount St.

118

Mary's College is built around Spinkhill Hall, a former home of the recusant Pole family and a boys' public school run by Jesuits. The Poles' private oratory was never discovered by the priest-hunters of the Reformation and after, and is still in use by the Jesuits today. Barlborough Hall (*vide* Barlborough) is the preparatory school for the College and only a short distance away.

The R.C. church near the College is a Puginesque building designed by Joseph Hansom in the 1840s. Hansom (1803-1882) was the inventor of the 'Patent Safety Cab' named after him. The broach spire is a well-known landmark.

The College itself has its own fine cruciform chapel with a dome over the crossing. It was designed by Adrian Gilbert Scott in the 1920s.

SPONDON *Map L.8*
See under Derby.

STANAGE EDGE *Map C.5*
ON THE Yorkshire border, the highest points of Stanage Edge are Stanage End (1,428 ft) and High Neb (1,502 ft).

STANLEY *Map K.8*
SIX MILES from Derby and eleven miles from Nottingham, the parish comprises Stanley village and Stanley Common. The church of St. Andrew has 14th century features but was heavily restored in 1874.

STANTON-BY-BRIDGE *Map N.7*
A TRIM little village on the south side of Swarkestone Bridge, with the Church of St. Michael showing structural evidence of Saxon work. A Norman chancel arch, window and doorway have been retained during several restorations. There is an incised monument to William Sacheverell. St. Bride's farm close by has a Norman tympanum.

STANTON-BY-DALE *Map L.9*
THE VILLAGE is unspoilt, providing a good example of the way in which a rural community can exist in harmony alongside large industrial developments. The small church of St. Michael and All Angels, dating from the thirteenth century, contains a register which dates from 1604 and is in a good state of preservation. Here is the fine Erewash Valley Golf Course.

STANTON-IN-THE-PEAK *Map F.5*
FINE ROCK scenery is to be found in this district. Stanton Hall is the seat of the Thornhill family (now Davie-Thornhill). North east are the scattered hamlets of Pilhough and Congreave, chiefly of farmhouses, one of which, Stanton Old Hall, is an interesting example of an old English farmstead. *The Flying Childers* public house is named after a champion race horse owned by the 4th Duke of Devonshire. The early Victorian church contains memorials to the Thornhills.

STANTON MOOR *Map G.5*
NOT VERY far from Birchover, on elevated ground above Darley Dale, which may be reached by road, Stanton Moor attracts considerable attention by reason of the prehistoric remains found here, the circle known as 'The Nine Ladies' and the masses of outcrop rock, including the 'Twopenny Loaf' 'Cork Stone', etc. The views are very fine. A square tower on the edge of the moor commemorates Earl Grey and the passing of the dreaded Reform Bill of 1832 and was put up by a member of the Thornhill family (see previous entry).

STAVELEY *Map E.8*
FOUR MILES from Chesterfield town centre, Staveley, a manufacturing and coalmining centre and part of Chesterfield borough, is situated in the midst of interesting countryside. The Chesterfield Canal passes through the parish. Staveley has an exceptionally fine church with many memorials to the Frecheville family. The register of the church dates from 1557 and the font is of Norman date. Other notable buildings include Staveley Hall (by John Smythson, c.1630, since reduced), the Staveley-Netherthorpe Grammar School and Hagge Farm, Handley. The founder of the famous Gisborne Charities, the Rev. Francis Gisborne, was Rector of Staveley; the Duke of Devonshire (Lord of the Manor), and St. John's College Cambridge, are the principal landowners. There is a public park with a well-equipped open-air swimming bath and a lake for fishing by permit holders. Other parks and playing fields are provided with children's playing equipment; in addition to a putting green there are bowling greens and tennis courts.

STEETLEY *Map D.10*
THIS VILLAGE contains what Dr. Pevsner, ignoring Melbourne, called 'by far the richest example of Norman architecture in Derbyshire'. Though only 52 ft long by 15 ft wide, Steetley Chapel has a lavish display of mid-twelfth century decoration and other features that make it an outstanding showpiece. There is another structure like it at Kilpeck in Worcestershire.

Steetley Chapel

Trees enfold this leafy corner of Stoney Middleton in high summer

STONEY MIDDLETON *Map E.5*

THE ROMANS are said to have had a settlement here and the site of a reputed Roman bath, fed by a thermal spring, lies behind the Hall, which was owned by the distinguished Judge, Lord Denham.

Its strange church, hidden away in the Nook, is said to be the only octagonal one in the country. Joan Padley built the first church here in the fifteenth century as a thanks-offering for delivering her spouse from death at the Battle of Agincourt. In the secluded square before the church two wells are blessed and dressed with flowers each year on the fourth Saturday in July.

STRETTON *Map G.8*

FIRST MENTIONED in 1002 as Straettum, it was later called Stratune in Domesday Book. Stretton is situated on the Roman Ryknield Street. Essentially an agricultural area, there is some beautiful scenery to be seen here. Handley and Woolley Moor are also in the parish.

SUDBURY *Map M.4*

A VICTORIAN photograph shows children playing in the main street and older people standing in the middle of the road gossiping. Such activities in the 1970s would have meant sudden death as this village straddled the main Derby to Stoke-on-Trent road and was perpetually choked with lorries and private motors. Now all is peace again. The by-pass has left Sudbury a much safer place and one can now better appreciate fine buildings such as *The Vernon Arms*, the Victorian butcher's shop and the school.

The 14th century church of All Saints stands back from the road in a lovely churchyard. It was restored in 1834 and again in 1874. There are some fine and interesting monuments to the Vernon family. Queen Victoria presented the east window in memory of a former rector who had served both the Queen and her Consort. A further window was inserted during the time when the Dowager Queen Adelaide lived at the Hall which is the main building of interest at Sudbury. For centuries it was the seat of the Lords Vernon until its transference to the National Trust.

SUDBURY HALL *Map M.4*. See page 22.

SURPRISE VIEW *Map D.5*
A SURPRISE indeed, this view-point appears suddenly on the main road from Sheffield to Hathersage and takes in a vast prospect over the wooded valley of the Derwent to the rugged uplands.

SUTTON-ON-THE-HILL *Map L.5*
A QUIET hamlet off the Derby-Uttoxeter road two miles north-west of Etwall. The tower and spire of St. Michael's Church at the top of the hill were rebuilt in 1831 and make a familiar landmark among a scattered agricultural community. Many years ago the family of

Chetham held the manorial rights and one member, Humphrey, founded and endowed the well-known Chetham Hospital and Library in Manchester. The Buckstons, formerly of Bradbourne Hall, own the wonderfully attractive gothick Hall, formerly the Vicarage, dating from 1819.

SUTTON SCARSDALE *Map F.8*
VISIBLE FROM the M1 near Heath are the extraordinary ruins of one of Derbyshire's grandest houses. The village is nothing out of the ordinary but close by and almost touching the little 14th century church are the remains of Sutton Scarsdale Hall, home of the Leakes, Earls of Scarsdale and later of the Arkwrights. The house was built to the designs of Smith of Warwick for the 1st Earl of Scarsdale (no connexion with the Curzons of Kedleston) and much important plasterwork was carried out by Venetian stuccoists, fragments of which survive.

The 1st Earl is supposed to have been taken by Hogarth as the model for the gouty old peer in his series *The Rake's Progress*. In turn, one of the later owners, an Arkwright, was supposed to have been the model for D. H. Lawrence's 'Sir Clifford Chatterley'.

The little church of St. Mary, described by Pevsner as 'Incongruously close to the Hall' is in fact a remarkable foil to its large neighbour (cf. Kedleston).

After decaying for some years the ruin was rescued, the very day before it was due to be pulled down completely, by the late Sir Osbert Sitwell who wanted the ruin preserved as a monument to Man's folly in allowing such objects of beauty to be destroyed. As

The Surprise View, a famous but unexpected sight for motorists on the A625

The ruin of Sutton Scarsdale. It can be seen from the M1

such it stands today, but now Sir Reresby Sitwell has placed it in the care of the D.o.E.

SWADLINCOTE *Map O.6*

SWADLINCOTE LIES in the extreme south-western part of Derbyshire which here projects like a promontory between Staffordshire to the west and Leicestershire to the east, with Burton-upon-Trent on the one hand and Ashby-de-la-Zouch on the other. The character of the town has changed considerably over the years, largely due to the natural resources of coal and clay in the district. Coal mining, clay extraction and manufacture of goods associated with this, and to a small extent, engineering, are the predominant industries of the district.

The British Coal Corporation's Central Engineering and Research Establishment is sited at Stanhope Bretby with a Test Site, where new plant and machinery are tested and proved.

New administrative offices within the Civic Centre house the Council Departments, while the South Derbyshire Leisure Centre, with swimming pool, learner pool, squash courts and a multi-purpose hall was opened in 1978. Further substantial improvements are planned. There are attractive well-laid out parks at Swadlincote, Church Gresley and Newhall, together with other facilities to meet the recreational needs of the residents. The church of St. George and St. Mary at Church Gresley was established in the 12th century by the Augustinian Canons.

SWANWICK *Map H.8*

THIS VILLAGE, pleasantly situated on high ground about midway between Alfreton and Ripley, is first mentioned in a Beauchief Abbey Charter of about 1275.

When stocking-weaving was introduced late in the eighteenth century it was at first a cottage industry, but later shops were built to accommodate several frames. In 1847 Stephen Elliott opened a workshop and soon gained a reputation for the quality of his stockings. A partnership was formed between Stephen Elliott and his sons, and shortly afterwards the firm of A. and C. Elliott began the manufacture of hand-made silk hosiery of superfine quality 'Patronised by Royalty and the Nobility'.

At the Delves there still stands the old endowed school, founded by Elizabeth Turner, of Swanwick Hall, in 1740 for the free education of 20 poor scholars.

The Church of St. Andrew was built in 1860 by private subscription and a generous donation from the Butterley Company. The tower, containing five bells, was built in 1903 by Fitzherbert Wright of The Hayes as a memorial to Queen Victoria. The venerable relic of domestic architecture in the village is the seventeenth century house in Wood's Yard, once the home of the Wathey family. The Hall, by Joseph Pickford, was built in 1776 for the Wood family.

The Conference Centre at The Hayes, Swanwick, has residential accommodation for over 300 delegates and is a popular centre for both national and international conferences, particularly for religious and welfare organisations.

SWARKESTONE *Map M.7*

THE BRIDGE over the Trent, three-quarters of a mile long, dates from the 14th century and at that time possessed a bridge chapel, one of three in Derbyshire. A pretty legend says that it was built by two sisters who lost their lovers during the floods, hence the chapel or chantry of intercession midway across the waters. This was the most southerly point reached by the advanced guard of Prince Charles Edward Stuart's army in 1745. It also saw battle in the Civil War, when Sir John Gell routed the Cavaliers in 1643. Good coarse fishing may be enjoyed in the Trent, and there are many pleasant walks in the neighbourhood of the river. Standing above in the meadows outside the village is the so-called Swarkestone Summer House, a

The Swarkestone Summer House

mysterious building, probably a relic of the huge seat of the Harpur family which was once close by and which was demolished when the family moved to Calke Abbey (q.v.) in the 17th century. It is now the property of the Landmark Trust.

The Derwent Sailing Club operates from the nearby gravel pits.

The tiny village clings to the North banks of the Trent. Its church contains magnificent alabaster effigies of members of the Harpur family.

TADDINGTON *Map E.3*

SITUATED IN the limestone centre of Derbyshire over 1,000 feet above sea level, this neighbourhood cannot fail to appeal to all who love the wild beauty of the hills and dales of the county. About one and a half miles from the village stands The Five Wells

Tumulus, one of the best examples of an ancient burial place now surviving. The old church of St. Michael's and All Angels has some interesting monuments and brasses, and the register dates from 1640. In the churchyard there is also an old cross shaft of uncertain antiquity. Pevsner wonders whether it is Norman.

TANSLEY *Map G.6*

1½ MILES east of Matlock this small village has remains of old industries, an 18th century mill and a tiny church in 1840 Early English style.

TAXAL *Map D.1*

'TINY, REMOTE, exceptionally beautiful and exceedingly silent' is how Roy Christian described the small hamlet near Whaley Bridge and the Goyt Valley. Until a few years back the landed family were the Jodrells who produced fighting men from Agincourt to the second World War. One of their estates, Jodrell Bank in Cheshire, now has quite different connotations. Their monuments are to be seen in the church together with one to Michael Heathcote 'Yeoman of the Mouth' to George II. This presumably meant that he was 'taster' to the King to prevent his royal master from being poisoned – a clear case for the payment of danger money.

Glebe Farm, Taxal Lodge and the Rectory are among the notable buildings in the village. Near-by Shallcross Hall has been demolished. See also Whaley Bridge.

TEMPLE NORMANTON *Map F.8*

ABOUT FOUR miles from Chesterfield on the Chesterfield-Mansfield road, this parish takes its name from the former preceptory of the Knights Templar.

The 18th century classical section of Swarkeston Bridge over the Trent

Thorpe Cloud

THORPE CLOUD *Map J.4*

A LIMESTONE hill at the southern entrance to Dovedale. The view of the dale is best seen from here. The path from the Peveril of the Peak Hotel across the fields leads to the summit. Immediately below, as one stands on the ridge at the top of Thorpe Cloud, is the grey-stone village of Thorpe, originally a Danish settlement. Its church has a Norman tower and nave. Two hotels and several farmhouses in the district offer good accommodation.

THREE SHIRES HEAD *Map F.1*

A DELIGHTFUL centre to which large numbers are always attracted by the fact that it is the meeting place of three counties – Derbyshire, Cheshire and Staffordshire. Pannier's Bridge used to be a favourite spot with pugilists in the old days. It is best reached by way of the Axe Edge road from Buxton or Leek.

THURVASTON *Map L.5*

IN A rich farmland area, this hamlet has a remarkable old oak tree which has stood for years without any sign of life. It would make a perfect setting for the Act 1, Scene 1 of 'Macbeth'.

TIBSHELF *Map G.8*

FORMERLY A prosperous coal-mining village but now with a rapidly expanding industrial estate, Tibshelf lies close to the Nottinghamshire border. The church is dedicated to St. John the Baptist and is a fine building with embattled tower and six bells. A one day flower show and sports event is held each year. One of the first land-based oil finds was made near here, some thirty years ago.

TICKNALL *Map N.7*

WITH A long, straggling village street in the more

mellow style found in the southern part of the county, Ticknall is at a convenient distance from despoiling coal measures a few miles away over the hill. St. George's Church was rebuilt in 1842, succeeding an earlier structure of which there are some remains in the churchyard. The fine old Vicarage is surrounded by modern housing on all sides. There is also a stone round house or 'lock-up'. Calke Abbey (q.v.) is near.

TIDESWELL *Map E.4*

TIDESWELL MAY well be termed a village of the mountain, for it lies in the midst of high limestone expanses on every side. Its church, known as 'The Cathedral of the Peak', was built entirely during the 14th century. Despite the apparent isolation of this little town the church contains some notable monuments, brasses and other relics of its ancient benefactors. The churchyard contains an old cross and sundial. Tideswell was granted a Market Charter in 1250. Tideswell Dale, which leads to Litton Mill, is a romantic spot once threaded by an old coach road. Tideswell is also renowned for its Wakes Week which begins on the nearest Saturday to 24th June each year. The Well-Dressing ceremony and Morris Dancing also take place at this time.

Near Wheston is the base of an ancient wayside cross, locally known as the 'Wishing Stone' and beyond the much reduced Wheston Hall is a fourteenth century cross with representations of the Nativity and Crucifixion. There is also the base of a cross at Butterton.

William Newton, 'the Minstrel of the Peak', was born in Tideswell in 1750, and is buried in the churchyard.

TINTWHISTLE *Map A.1*

FORMERLY IN Cheshire, but now part of Derbyshire, this village is close to the Manchester reservoirs in the

The famous Church of St. John the Baptist at Tideswell, rich in pre-Reformation monuments

Tissington Hall, seat of the Fitzherberts. Opposite: the village of Tissington

valley of the River Etherow in Longdendale. The church was built in 1837. A legend tells of Dick Turpin reversing his horse's shoes hereabouts to put his pursuers off the trail.

TISSINGTON *Map H.4*

AS NEAR perfection as you can get – except when teeming with people on a hot summer day. When approaching from the Ashbourne-Buxton road one enters gates guarded by a lodge at the head of a tree-lined avenue as if approaching a country house. Instead of a solitary manor house the drive leads to a whole community which seems to have grown haphazardly around the great house of the FitzHerberts. Tissington Hall is the focal point of the village and has been a seat of the FitzHerberts for half a millenium, though the present house is 17th century. It is not open to the public.

The church stands on high ground, a little removed from the scattered houses of the village and its wide thoroughfare. It contains many monuments to the FitzHerberts.

Tissington is famous as being the mother-place of the ancient and mysterious ceremony of well-dressing. It is known that wells were dressed here in 1350 but the custom probably dates from before the Romans. The ceremony takes place on Ascension Day each year and six wells are dressed and blessed.

The Tissington Trail set up by the Peak National Park is a scenic route 13 miles in length, running from Ashbourne to Parsley Hay. The trail follows the old Buxton to Ashbourne railway and the rambler or rider finds himself travelling through the matchless countryside of the National Park without the interference of cars, pollution or noise. There are car-parking points for people joining the trail at various stages. Walking and cycling routes, all clearly signposted, take the visitor to various local places of interest. There are also shorter routes for people who do not wish to wander too far: these are circular routes based on several of the car parks along the White Peak Scenic Route. At Hartington the old signal box is now an Information Point, open in summer on Saturdays, Sundays and Bank Holidays.

The High Peak Trail offers the same facilities and in fact joins up with the Tissington Trail at Parsley Hay, where there are lavatories for the disabled. The High Peak, however, is 17½ miles long and follows the old Cromford and High Peak Railway, starting at Cromford and finishing at Dowlow, south of Buxton.

Cyclists need not necessarily bring their own bikes as there is a hire service available between April and October. A returnable deposit is required and the bicycles for hire can be found at Parsley Hay car park (just off the A.515 approximately twelve miles from

The Hall Well, Tissington at well-dressing time (see Derbyshire Customs – page 26). Left: Tissington Trail

Ashbourne), at Middleton Top and at Ashbourne (close to the swimming pool).

Leaflets giving details of cycle hire and routes for the walker and cyclist can also be obtained from these centres.

TOAD'S MOUTH *Map D.5*

CLOSE TO the road between Longshaw Lodge and Hathersage with wild Burbage Moor to the north stands one of Nature's own non-abstract sculptures – the Toad's Mouth – an extraordinary and solitary rock sitting by the roadside for all the world like Beatrix Potter's 'Mr. Jackson'. If you first see this giant amphibian in stone on the way to Hathersage and are surprised by it, there is a bigger surprise a little further along the road when it suddenly turns sharply to the right to reveal the 'Surprise View' (q.v.).

The Toad's Mouth

TRENT LOCK *Map M.9*

WHILST MANY of the canals of the county are becoming neglected it is pleasing to note a growing interest awakening to protect and use those which are left. It was James Brindley, a son of Derbyshire, who exercised so much engineering skill to join together the River Trent with the River Mersey and thus connected the two coasts by inland waterways. Sir Richard Arkwright who built the first cotton mill in the world, at Cromford, gave his support to the building of the Cromford Canal which connected with the Erewash Canal and then joined the River Trent at Trent Lock.

TRUSLEY *Map L.5*

THE SMALL brick All Saints Church (1713), contains

A wonderful place for messing about in boats. A scene at Trent Lock

contemporary box pews and a three-decker pulpit. The Coke-Steel family is seated here.

TUPTON *Map F.8*
A RESIDENTIAL parish about four miles south of Chesterfield.

TURNDITCH *Map J.6*
IN THE lovely Ecclesbourne valley, Turnditch lies just off the Wirksworth-Duffield road.

TUTBURY *Map M.5*
A SMALL town just over the Staffordshire border. Its broad main street is one of perfect architectural harmony between Tudor, Georgian and Victorian buildings and has been designated a conservation area.

Not a great deal remains of Tutbury Castle, one of the melancholy prisons of Mary Stuart

The principal feature is the 12th century castle, the ruins of which perch 100 feet above the plain below the town. It was one of several places where Mary Queen of Scots was imprisoned and in the next century it was a Royalist stronghold in the Civil War though reduced by Cromwellian cannon. It is regularly open to the public.

Also in an elevated position in the town is the parish church of St. Mary, dating from the 1080s and partly restored by the great Victorian architect G. E. Street.

Tutbury is also known for its crystal cut glass, and at Chapman's Sheepskins it is often possible to see sheepskins being washed, cleaned, tanned, stretched and dried before being combed and finished.

TWO DALES *Map G.6*
BETWEEN Matlock and Rowsley is Two Dales – situated along the southern bank of the Sydnope

Valley. Knab Rocks, sheer gritstone cliffs, are on the opposite side of the valley. The district is well-known for its rhododendron bushes. Sydnope Hall was once the home of the antiquary Sir Francis Sacheverell Darwin.

TWYFORD *Map M.6*
LIKE SWARKESTONE, Twyford lies close to the banks of the River Trent. Also like Swarkestone the 14th century church with its Georgian nave contains monuments to the Harpurs. The Hall is a pretty house on the river's edge: a ferry once plied across the Trent here.

VIA GELLIA *Map H.5, 6*
BETWEEN Cromford and Grangemill is a ravine some two miles in length along which in the 18th century Philip Gell, of Hopton Hall, Wirksworth, constructed a drive and gave it the name Via Gellia, perhaps an oblique reference to the Gells' alleged Roman descent. The trade name 'Viyella' is derived from this as a textile mill in the Via Gellia once produced this fabric.

House above the Via Gellia constructed in tufa, a kind of rock formed from dissolved limestone which has been redeposited in water

WALTON-ON-TRENT *Map O.5*
CHURCH WITH early English chancel and fifteenth century tower, contains some Norman features. A fine brass of Robert Morley, Rector (died 1492) and modern woodwork and glass in the east window are worthy of note.

WARDLOW *Map E.4*
THIS VILLAGE is situated on the road that runs between Longstone Moor on the one side and Wardlow Hay Cop (1,216 ft) on the other.

WATERHOUSES *Map J.2*

THE MANIFOLD TRACK, a trail following the line of the former Manifold Valley Light Railway, leads from a car park and picnic site in the village through lovely country to Hulme End.

WELLINGTON MONUMENT *Map E.5*

THIS CONSPICUOUS monument, erected about 1866 in honour of the Iron Duke, may be seen on the moors above Baslow and Calver. The site commands wide views over the Derwent valley.

WENSLEY *Map G.5*

CLOSE TO Winster, Birchover, Darley Dale and the Matlocks, this district is popular with walkers for Wensley lies in a particularly scenic part of the county.

WESSINGTON *Map G.7*

A RURAL parish situated 2½ miles north west of Alfreton. The village centres round a wide green and its old pub *The Horse and Jockey*. The parish's five miles of footpaths and bridleways offer walks through attractive countryside.

WEST HALLAM *Map K.8*

THOUGH adjacent to expanding Ilkeston, it still retains something of its old charm. The church of St. Wilfred contains 14th century work but its most notable features are the monuments and in particular the canopied effigies of Walter Powtrell who died in 1598 and his wife Cassandra Shirley.

WESTON UNDERWOOD *Map K.6*

ADJOINING THE Kedleston estate, this village is the centre of a strong agricultural community. There is also a large prestressed concrete works nearby.

WESTON-UPON-TRENT *Map M.8*

THIS ATTRACTIVE village possesses a prettily sited church dedicated to St. Mary with features of the 13th and 14th centuries and a 17th century parish bier. The register dates from 1565 and in the churchyard lie soldiers who fell in the Civil War. There is good fishing in the canal, which lies just below the *Cliff Inn*, now the *Old Cliff House*. Weston Hall is prominently sited but only half the size it was intended. The Ropers started it in 1633 but the Civil War put paid to its completion.

WETTON *Map H.3*

GROUPED AROUND its village inn and the part 14th century church, this pleasant stone-built village stands high above Wetton Mill in the Manifold Valley. Nearby is the spectacular Thor's Cave and the area is of outstanding natural beauty and archaeological interest.

WHALEY BRIDGE *Map D.1*

WHALEY BRIDGE is a typical small North Country town on the western edge of the Peak District National Park. A by-pass now skirts the town centre and the principal thoroughfare, Market Street, is part of the old Manchester to Buxton Road. Here is situated a selection of shops and the public library.

Another popular boating centre is the canal wharf at Whaley Bridge, a few miles from Manchester

The Memorial Park is in the town centre with playing fields, tennis courts and a bowling green nearby.

Although textile and other mills operate in the town they do not impinge upon the essentially rural nature of the area. The Goyt Valley is a natural beauty spot with the woods and stream winding south towards Buxton. Adjacent, are a score of other woodland retreats of great natural beauty, whilst two large reservoirs give vistas of a different sort. On every side are the hills of the Peak, including Eccles Pike and the more distant ranges of Kinder Scout, whilst to the west the more gentle Cheshire uplands are to be seen. For the hiker or country-lover, Whaley Bridge is an ideal centre. The Peak Forest canal terminates here in a small basin where there is a base for hiring cruisers, and a small museum and art gallery.

Early in the nineteenth century cotton mills were built at Taxal and the first of these was described by Linnaeus Banks in *A Manchester Man*.

Originally of the twelfth century, St. James's Church was mostly rebuilt in 1825 although, fortunately, the attractive castellated sixteenth century tower survives in its original form. The church has six bells, two of which are pre-Reformation. In the chancel there are epitaphs to the Jodrells of near-by Yeardsley Hall, one of whom fought at Agincourt. Their old family home was at Taxal (q.v.).

WHATSTANDWELL *Map H.7*

THERE IS no more picturesque section of the Derwent Valley than the stretch of the A6 road from Cromford and the Matlocks to Whatstandwell. This is an excellent fishing centre and there are fine walks in all directions. The Shining Cliff Woods were presented to the National Trust by Alderman J. G. Graves, of Sheffield. Alport Height (1,034 ft) stands to the south.

WHESTON *Map D.3*
See under Tideswell.

WHITTINGTON *Map E.7*
A SUBURB of Chesterfield now but containing several interesting buildings, including the Victorian church of St. Bartholomew and Revolution House (formerly the Cock and Pynot Inn) where Lord Devonshire and others plotted to replace Catholic James II with his Protestant daughter and son-in-law William of Orange and Mary. This is now a museum.

Revolution House, Whittington

WHITWELL *Map D.10*
A VILLAGE on the county boundary, in an agricultural area, with some coalmining and quarrying activity. St. Lawrence Church at Whitwell dates back as far as 1150 and the register from 1672. Sir Roger Manners, who died in 1632, has his monument here, not far from his home of Whitwell Manor, part of which is now the Parish Hall. On the Sunday nearest to St. Lawrence's Day an annual service is held in a quarry

Willington Power Station, one of several utilising the waters of the River Trent, has a dramatic beauty of its own

on High Hill. The very fine old Whitwell Wood is some 440 acres in extent. The poet John William Streets, who was killed in the Battle of the Somme, was a native of Whitwell, one of the large family of a coal miner. A short distance away is Steetley Chapel (q.v.).

WILLINGTON *Map N.6*
ONE MILE from Repton, this village is on the banks of the Trent. The church was rebuilt in the 19th century and contains a Norman south doorway. The five-arch bridge was one of the last to escape the payment of tolls. The toll board hangs in the porch of St. Wystan's Church at Repton.

WILNE *Map M.8*
See under Draycott.

WINDLEY *Map K.6*
A VILLAGE almost buried in the lush countryside close to the Ecclesbourne Valley. The Hall, once the property of the Cromptons, is a handsome building, and at the end of a long drive at the other end of the village is Flower Lilies, another large house which once belonged to the banker J. G. Crompton who was driven in a pony trap every morning to Hazelwood Station in the 1870s. If he were late, the train would not leave without him.

Hereabout are bred shire-horses and on the first Saturday of September each year there is a gymkhana and flower show.

WINGERWORTH *Map F.7*
CLOSE BY Chesterfield, Wingerworth's great house has gone but it has a Parish Church of Norman origins in which fine old wall-paintings have been discovered and renovated. The Church, All Saints,

Tombstone in Wingerworth churchyard

has in recent years been enlarged. The Norman south door and the Anglian arches lead to a modern cruck style interior. The ancient chancel arch overlooked by the rood loft and stairs encloses the Lady Chapel.

The Parish is mainly rural in character and has pleasant hill and woodland scenery. There are playing fields, open spaces and a fine new Village Hall.

WINGFIELD MANOR *Map H.7*
See under South Wingfield.

WIN HILL *Map C.4*
1,523 FOOT high Win Hill was called by Ebenezer Elliott, the 'Corn-Law ryhmer', the 'Eldest Brother of the Air and Light'. Lying north-east of Hope a footpath from the Hope-Edale road through Twitchill Farm passes close to the summit and then descends to Ashley Farm.

THE WINNATS *Map C.3*
THE NAME Winnats means 'Wind Gates' and this mountain pass on the road between Chapel-en-le-Frith and Castleton is certainly notorious for its howling winds. Only light traffic may use the Pass.

WINSTER *Map G.5*
AN ANCIENT market town that still has a curfew bell which rings at eight in the evening (sometimes at seven); it also has a bell that rouses one at six o'clock in the morning! Traditionally pancake races are held on Shrove Tuesday every year. Winster was one of the five chapels given, in the reign of Henry II, to the Abbey of Leicester, along with the mother church at Youlgreave. There are some interesting late-seventeenth-century houses. At the Hall lived Llewellyn Jewitt, the Derbyshire historian and local archaeo-

Winnats Pass, a beautiful natural gorge near Castleton, which was probably once a cavern

132

Winster, showing the old Market House

logist. The building is now a public house and during conversion work a frescoed ceiling was discovered. The Market House is an interesting survival. Since 1906 it has belonged to the National Trust and now serves as the Trust's information centre.

WIRKSWORTH *Map H.6*

THERE IS nothing quite like Wirksworth in the British Isles. This down-to-earth quarry town is, on the face of it, dusty, noisy and bustling. Yet off the main road are many enchanting little streets and alleyways giving vistas of roofscapes and surrounding green hills. In the centre, little has changed except for the pre-War demolition of a couple of houses in the former Market Place to allow the main road to proceed swiftly through the town. So far tourism has not ruined its unique character.

Wirksworth has had its share of housing development, mostly to the south, but once in the heart of the place it is all enchantment. A few years ago it was in a state of some decline but a new sense of civic pride has swept through the town due largely to a revitalising Project by the Civic Trust, Sainsbury's Wirksworth Project and the Derbyshire Historic Buildings Trust. For the Heritage Centre, see p. 7.

'The oldest firm in Wirksworth' is how some wag described the tremendously grand parish church of St. Mary which proudly proclaims on its church board that it was founded (as indeed it was) in AD 653. Inside will be found fragments of that earlier Saxon church including one of the country's most important pieces of Anglo-Saxon sculpture – a coffin

'George Eliot'

133

St. Mary's Church, Wirksworth, which stands in a wide circle of buildings somewhat resembling a cathedral close. The Gell Almshouses are to the right

Left: Chancel windows of Wirksworth Church showing arms of Hurt, Fownes and Lowe

lid elaborately carved to represent events in the life of Christ. The circular churchyard and houses around suggest a cathedral close rather than the parish church of a smallish town. The reason is that Wirksworth was at one time a much more important place than it is today, being a centre of the lead-mining industry since Roman times. Barmote Courts are still held to discuss lead-mining matters in the Moot Hall. The old Grammar School building in the churchyard is now the home and workshop of a craftsman in wood. Founded by Anthony Gell in the 16th century the school is now a large comprehensive. Gell, along with other members of his family (*vide* Hopton) are buried in the church and their fine monuments can be seen. Anthony Gell also founded the attractive almshouses facing the church.

A very rare custom takes place here annually – the famous 'Clypping' of the church – a practical demonstration of affection for the building by the parishioners who actually 'embrace' the church by surrounding it. Well-dressing also takes place on the Saturday before Spring Bank Holiday. The town has strong connexions with George Eliot being the 'Snowfield' in her novel *Adam Bede*.

WOODVILLE *Map O.6*
A MODERN parish near the Leicestershire border, it is notable for its industry. Norman style church of 1846.

WORMHILL *Map E.3*
HERE William Bagshawe, Apostle of the Peak, preached his first sermon in the village closely associated with the Bagshawe family. Wormhill is also the birthplace of James Brindley the canal pioneer. Lying in a hollow in the Peak, Wormhill has a lovely old stone gabled Hall of Elizabethan times still the home of the Bagshawes.

WYASTON *Map K.4*
A HAMLET just off the Ashbourne-Sudbury road and close to Osmaston, Wyaston typifies the farming land of middle-west Derbyshire.

YEAVELEY *Map K.4*
THE VILLAGE is said to have been the birthplace of one of the greatest architects of the Middle Ages whose name we know – Henry Yevele who worked on Canterbury Cathedral and Westminster Abbey. The little village church is entirely of 1840 and one of the few brick churches in this part of the world. It replaced an earlier building, of which the medieval font is the only survival.

The real importance of Yeaveley is to be found down a muddy track outside the village – 'a remote and altogether mysterious place' was how Henry Thorold described it. This is Stydd Hall, an Elizabethan house originally closely akin to North Lees Hall (p. 87) with 19th century Gothick additions. Built on much earlier foundations, this building is now a farmhouse but its earlier significance can be seen in the garden where are the remains of a 13th century chapel with elegant lancet windows. This served what was once a preceptory or community of Knights Hospitallers of St. John of Jerusalem of which Stydd Hall was once part. This Order rivalled the Knights Templars and was active during the Crusades. Its headquarters were at Acre. It is strange to come upon this dramatic relic of the Age of Chivalry in deepest Derbyshire.

The ruined chapel at Stydd

YOULGREAVE *Map F.5*
AN ANCIENT upland village in the midst of fine limestone scenery. Youlgreave (often spelt as it is pronounced Youlgrave) is perched on the edge of Bradford Dale and quite close to the lovely Lathkill Dale. The church has some fine Norman work and a beautiful table tomb with an effigy of Thomas Cockayne. The stained glass is by Kempe with the exception of the east windows which are the work of William Morris and Burne-Jones. There is an aisle dedicated, at the behest of H. S. Wheatly-Crowe, the well-known protagonist of Charles I, to the Martyr King. The banner he presented to the church in 1904 is now displayed in the aisle, and he is buried in the churchyard.

A village of distinct character, it forms an ideal setting for the old custom of Well-Dressing and a ceremony is held on the Saturday before the nearest Sunday to St. John the Baptist's Day, when a procession threads through the village led by the uniformed brass band.

Youlgreave

Published by Derbyshire Countryside Ltd., Lodge Lane, Derby.

Photography by Andy Williams, R. L. Moore, Mike Williams, Frank Rodgers, C. A. Bonser, John Colley, Brian Lawrence, Roy Deeley, Newbery Smith Photography Ltd., Vernon D. Shaw, E. A. Woodall, G. Bryan Allsop, James Behrendt, S. C. Sedgwick and Jeremy Whitaker.

The Long Gallery at Sudbury Hall and the High Great Chamber at Hardwick are by courtesy of the National Trust. The portrait of Jedediah Strutt is by courtesy of the Derby City Art Gallery and that of Wright of Derby by permission of Mr. C. H. Rogers-Coltman.

The photographs of Bolsover Castle and Chesterfield Market Place are by courtesy of the D.o.E and Chesterfield Borough Council.

D. H. Lawrence by Jack Bronson is by courtesy of Moorley's of Ilkeston and the picture of Renishaw Hall and the Sargent group of the Sitwell family are by courtesy of Sir Reresby and Lady Sitwell. The Editor would like to thank Mr. Maxwell Craven, Keeper of Antiquities, Derby Museum, for his invaluable help over architectural matters, Mrs. Shelagh Johnson and the many others who have been helpful in one way or another.

ISBN 0 85100 109 2

INDEX TO PLACES (Map references are shown in italics)